That Mind of Ours

Written by

John B. Lester

Copyright 2017 by John B. Lester

All rights reserved. Published in the United States by John B. Lester, a division of Team Prosper

ISBN: 0692080090
ISBN- 13: 9780692080092

IT GIVES ME PLEASURE AS WELL AS A SENSE OF ACCOMPLISH TO HAVE COMPLETED AND PUBLISHED MY FIRST BOOK. OFFICIALLY MAKING THE TRANSITION FROM A WRITER WITH LIMITLESS POTENTIAL TO AN AUTHOR WITH REQUIRED EXPECTATIONS. THE VISION BEHIND MY BOOK I PRESENT TO YOU TODAY CAN BE DESCRIBED BEST BY TELLING YOU THE STORY BEHIND THE STORYBOOK.

A

John B Lester

THAT MIND OF OURS

"Never let other people's expectations limit your capabilities"

John B. Lester

A dedication to those special friendships found in the most unlikely places, under the least likely situations.

John B Lester

THAT MIND OF OURS

A FEW FORWARD WORDS

The bible scriptures were difficult to understand. School books never held my interest. Comic books were taught never to be taken seriously. For me, the only consistency I found in reading was lip reading. I suppose you might call it reading between the lines of what was said.

Nevertheless, what conversation would be worth speaking unless we could speak our minds freely, rather than thinking of what we should say. To

John B Lester

THAT MIND OF OURS

engage in the art of free speech that comes at a mere cost of a penny for each other's thoughts. Because nothing in life is entirely free. Especially freedom. More lives have been lost fighting for freedom since the first languages were formed. And even that was only to determine who would be free and who would have to fight for their freedom. Now that's at least one open discussion everyone can agree on. Everybody wants freedom and loves the feeling of being free. Wouldn't you agree? Sometimes talking freely about anything can lead to something. Remember those two Jewish guys from New York who sat in a coffee shop all day talking

John B Lester

THAT MIND OF OURS

about nothing? Well for them that nothing certainly turned out to be quite something. For ten years the cast of Seinfeld made the world laugh at the everyday things most of us thought nothing of. It was one of the last real-life series before television became a series of unrealistic reality shows. A time when our free speech became limited as more free choice words became costly to say. One by one our politically correct dictionary dictators shamed some of most commonly used words into fearful whispers. The words in our language were slowly being dwindled down as if our language was dying from a form of a deadly verbal virus from the history

THAT MIND OF OURS

of the F word to the evolution of the N word. Whether it was politically speaking or speaking about pornography. The talk of any town was always about who's fucking who and who getting fucked by who. Our conversations were slowly becoming like sex. They were no longer safe unless you knew the correct words to protect yourself. Despite the fact, even the most politically incorrect dialogue dictators found it most difficult to take away America's favorite F words. Free and Freedom. Nevertheless, no matter who was fighting over what was language was right, or who was using the wrong language. To be able to keep any type of speech free, is to

John B Lester

THAT MIND OF OURS

empower our words instead of finding ways to shame them. Words are like our own personal set of keys. We never realize how important they are until we can't right find the right ones to use. Wouldn't you agree?

Officially I suppose this article will be labeled as my first blog post. Unofficially trading my self-proclaimed title as a life storyteller for one that labels me a writer. Nonetheless, I accept these terms as personal binding agreement that allows me the rights to convert the years of my life into chapters worthy to be in some form of publication. Although I can't help but already feel the burden of being my

THAT MIND OF OURS

own biggest critic. Somehow, I can already sense how the minds of writers struggle to find the perfect words to share with the world. Seems so ironic how some of the greatest writers end up isolating themselves into a world of their own. Now there's a fact that brings a thought to my mind. Would that be considered an afterthought or a fact for thought? No free-spirited thinker should have to be bear burden of solace to exercise their rights to free speech. Am I right? Although some of them might justify their time of just solitaire by taking the company of Jack Daniel or Mary Jane. Not that there is anything wrong with that. It just seems that most of their

John B Lester

THAT MIND OF OURS

biographies never end very well. What kind of retirement package is that anyway for someone who spends their career writing happy endings? Seems fitting they should deserve a happy ending of their own. I have make certain to inquire about that clause should I ever consider working for the Writers Union. Nonetheless, this is precisely the reason I believe this form of open minded writing that makes my open book is quite fitting to be called That Mind of Mine. Having just started newly claim status as a blogger a mere paragraph ago I wouldn't feel deserving to be referred to as a writer for at least six months or 100,000 words, perhaps less depending

John B Lester

THAT MIND OF OURS

on the quality of those words. Hopefully in time I will be able to tell before my readers have a chance to tell me. Can some blogs become a book just by writing a book blogs? Has the blogging community earned equal status among publishing companies?

John B Lester

THAT MIND OF OURS

Simplicity of Numbers

Studies have suggested that men predominantly use the right side of their brain while women use more of the left side. A trait which offers an explanation as to why men excel higher at math while women perform better in the languages. Although most people seem to agree that men's thought process comes from an entirely different part of the anatomy. Nevertheless, this theory might explain why most men have such trouble

THAT MIND OF OURS

understanding what women tell them. It might also explain men's fixation with numbers of sexual partners either side of the party had accumulated. Perhaps years of strategizing ways to score developed into their need to keep track of points. Hence eventually developing the instinct which views sex as a sport and women as the opponent. Leaving their hearts with only enough room for the love of the game. No matter whose opinion you may agree with most, there is no doubt that Darwin's theory of evolution is taking the next step as we speak. Time are shifting. People are evolving. Whether you're a people lover or a lover of the game

John B Lester

THAT MIND OF OURS

there is a new hope for love. Because this game is drastically changing. For example, by today's game time standards no woman should have any shame in having 39 points Perhaps the latest Cosmopolitan polls have increased that number to 49. In that case would 69 still be considered acceptable? My hope is that any woman (or man) at this point has come to realize (some pun intended) that there is no any logic behind numbers for that game. Not that there is anything wrong with those who choose to savor their domain as if it were a fine wine. Those Chardonnay sipping groupies are aware of the pleasures of sexual solitude. Which is why it makes

John B Lester

THAT MIND OF OURS

no sense for any of them to whine about those wanting to share theirs. Although, it was never the ignorant people who expressed their opinions that baffled me. It was the open-minded people who enjoyed sex that allowed themselves to be hindered and shamed by those who clearly needed to have a few organisms themselves. Otherwise, they would not get so uptight whenever the topic came up. Rather than exploring each other in their own adventures of bedroom diversity. Funny how something as simple as this could be such a touchy topic for some people. Yes, much pun intended. Objectively speaking I am aware there are people

John B Lester

THAT MIND OF OURS

who have certain rules, guidelines, even opinions that may differ from mine. I wouldn't expect anyone to break any rules, I would only hope they would question why the rules are in place. Perhaps, I can reiterate this type of thought processing by going back to our basics. A time when things were simple. It was the age of six when I was first enlightened by a simple concept. In fact, this might be something that just about everyone could agree on.

John B Lester

THAT MIND OF OURS

Seven Year Itch

The first six years of our lives were the days when each day was truly a new day. Each new sight was equally as grand as the next. Each new vision within our eyes sight was equally mesmerizing. Every freshly new thought was based on the perception of our own eyes. Each day was a world full of magic. A series of conquering wonderous boundaries. Every obstacle was overcome fearlessly. While each problem was solved with simplicity.

John B Lester

THAT MIND OF OURS

Then came 1st grade. Gradually we were told it was just a dream. It was only a movie. Magic was make believe. Ghost wasn't real. Stories were just fairy tales and tall legends.

By 6th grade you were taught what not to do. Where not to go. What not to talk about. Until anything outside a small window of creativity was told that it was only in our imagination.

By time we were 16. Our world had tunneled down to a few select paths we needed to choose from. Perhaps another reason three 6 's was considered cursed numbers

"Our bodies go through significant transitions every

THAT MIND OF OURS

seven years". Having just turned seven the previous summer, those words remained with me throughout the entire second grade. Leaving me to wonder what was so significant that came from being seven. It would be five cycles later before I put much thought into that statement. The age of 35 was the first time I heard the term, 7-year itch. A time I departed my longest relationship. A time when life had once again left me wondering where life's next significant transition would take me. Then somewhere along my timeline during that sixth cycle of life, that statement finally began to make some sense. Seven years is the time needed for one to learn the more important things in life. Only sometimes during that time, one might forget about the things that

John B Lester

THAT MIND OF OURS

were most important to them. Perhaps it is one of those thoughts that only appears simple at six.

If seven years is enough to break down our thoughts on some of life's simpler things. Then perhaps, it might be long enough to heal a broken heart too. I am not certain if the phrase forgive and forget derives from this type of thinking. Yet I do know that the seven-year forgiveness is an idea that comes from the Jewish custom. One which the 7-year bankruptcy term originates from. So, here is my thought. Does that entitle anyone to a clean slate.? Would that make everyone home free? How free would one really be? In my mind, would that make anyone free if they were merely back where they started. Wondering what significant changes had occurred during their past

John B Lester

THAT MIND OF OURS

cycle. Just like that curious 7-year-old boy scratching his head wondering what really changed. Personally, I like the Jewish philosophy which comes with one other stipulation. One that is based on their honor system which one agrees to payback life by mentoring someone else with their gained knowledge. That type of thinking I can truly appreciate. The idea of genuine collaboration. And with that type of thinking, I can really appreciate the significance in behind the cycle of life. Come to think of it, that type of thinking would essentially make me believe that my next cycle just might be the most fun years to come. And come to think of it ,the most famous number in baseball was number 7, worn by New York Yankee's legendary Mickey Mantle. Anyone will tell you he wasn't

John B Lester

THAT MIND OF OURS

best all time Yankee, but he known for being the one who had the most fun. After all, he does hold the title as the all-time greatest switch hitter. I supposed that's a special title within a league of its own. One that comes with being able to view the field from both sides of the plate.

The Choose My Own Adventure Begins

The hardest thing I had to adjust was always being scolded whenever I truly spoke my mind. My mind was always full of questions, wonders, and reminiscences. I still remember the first time Sister Mary-Louise made the announcement.

"Today is a special day for all of you because you will be going to the library and choosing any two books you wish to read. Once you finish reading

John B Lester

THAT MIND OF OURS

them, you will tell the whole class all about it. During your time here, Miss Tammy will be your librarian to help you find your books. Her job is quite special because she needs to know where each book belongs. "

While all the fourth graders awaited quietly in line, I had wondered off in between the first two aisles of books that seemed to tower pass the ceilings. It fascinated me how each title was placed perfectly in alphabetical order. I was so enticed by the endless choices of titles, I failed to noticed Father Michaels entrance into the library.

CLASS:

THAT MIND OF OURS

Good Morning Father Michaels. May the Lord be with you.

FATHER MICHAEL:

And may the Lord be with you as well.

Unaware of his presence behind me, I turned around and looked at him staring down on me." Are you enjoying the library JOHN?"

"Yes, Father. Do you have a favorite book?" I replied excitedly. Father Michael didn't respond., Instead he gave me a stern look as I noticed the rest of my classmates eyeing me nervously.

FATHER MICHAEL

"Were you told you could leave the line?"

John B Lester

THAT MIND OF OURS

I quickly responded with an answer I thought would be most appropriate. "Well. Father, Miss Tammie didn't tell us not to leave the line, but she tell us that when Gods speaks to us we should listen and follow with our heart." Somehow my answer was perceived in a mocking matter, resulting my recess privileges denied for the entire week. Fortunately, I did not mind the extra time to read his first two books. Firstly, The Life of Dr. Martin Luther King. Secondly, The Choose Your Own Adventure Book.

SIX FLAGS. JACKSON NEW JERSEY MAY 11,1984

John B Lester

THAT MIND OF OURS

Father Michael had a reputation as being a fierce figure of authority who was always angry. His weekday sermons were fueled with angered words on how mankind will face an eternity of suffering. Most of the others had disregarded his emotional rants by whispering to each other or fidgeting through the church's weekly pamphlets. I was dazzled watching him transcend into his story as if he was reliving it at that very moment., I thought that if I ever had the courage to tell a story in front of a church I hoped to do it as well as he did. After a while I slowly began telling people around me some of the stories I found most amusing to my surprise, it

John B Lester

THAT MIND OF OURS

seemed that people were enjoying my storytelling. Except for a few not so very nice boys that happened to be quite bigger than me. AMY

Don't let them make you afraid. They just bullies.

My emotions were never strong enough not to let it bother me. "Why does it seem that whenever good men speak like they are always getting punished or killed?"

AMY

"Maybe you just need to stop being such a wimp."

I sat on the far sidewalk from the recess area, listening to the church's afternoon bells tolling over me as I thought to myself," Maybe there is a good

John B Lester

THAT MIND OF OURS

reason why Father Michael was always so angry"
The day had arrived for the altar boy's annual trip to Great Adventure, A rewarding day free to do as we wished until our 3pm return time back at the bus. I still remember seeing the nearby clock display the time 2:12. We had enough time for one last stop at the Haunted House. Father Michael came raging toward the front of the line demanding we immediately return to the bus. Disgruntled by the unexplained exit that shortened our day we sat in silence as the bus began to motion. A moment later everyone was turning around to look out the bus's rear window. The entire bus of students and staff

John B Lester

THAT MIND OF OURS

watched in awe at the flaming tunnel of black smoke rising, just a short distance away.

Later that evening, I sat with my father watching the evening news repeated reports about a fire inside Great Adventure's haunted house. One that tragically killed 30 people that afternoon at 2:45. My father stared aimlessly at the television as I retold him the stories of the day. Somehow, I knew that day was not his first time experiencing a near lost.

John B Lester

THAT MIND OF OURS

The First Boss

Being deaf never seemed to be an indifference. The only notable difference from other pre-teen adolescents was a lack of interest in music listening. Perhaps the inability to hear any of the words being sung made music undesirable. Until one day I heard a song playing on the radio in my Uncle's woodshop. It had a beat that gravitated me closer to the speakers and made me feel like moving around. Each day afterwards I returned to my uncle's workshops after school and waited for the

John B Lester

THAT MIND OF OURS

popular hit to replay on the radio. No day was complete until I walked out of that workshop humming the words, Born in the USA. A few weeks later my mother called me into the living room and introduced me to the man on the radio who struck my musical interest. A man with whitewash denim jeans, short hair, no makeup, and no tattoos by the name of Bruce along with his merry E street band members. It was the first time I knew who the Boss was and the first time I knew the TV channels went higher than 20 on the cable box. That following Christmas my uncle gifted me my first cassette tape. Born in the USA. For the next 3-4 years the

John B Lester

THAT MIND OF OURS

only songs I listened to were on side A of that cassette. It wouldn't be until nearly 2 decades later until I would learn any of the words being played on my Walkman each night before I went to sleep.

My return to 6th grade was filled with post-holiday high spirit in hopes of bonding with classmates through a shared interest in music. Certain that my new denim jean jacket, red bandana, along with my Born in the USA cassette cover would surely win me some school yard acceptance. Unfortunately, that day would result in one of life's tough lessons. That day I learned that it was uncool to like Bruce Springsteen music. It was cool to like Poison, Metal,

John B Lester

THAT MIND OF OURS

Ratt, Twisted Sister and a man name Ozzy. I learned it was better to have no opinion and be rejected than to have a wrong opinion and to be ridiculed. It wouldn't until 4 more years before I knew any of those terms. However, I quickly learned that men who sang with makeup and long hair were most cool. In that same week, I learned that parents strongly disapproved of their children listening to any music from long haired men. Children were also restricted from hanging pictures of these long-haired men on their bedroom walls. This was a time I waited for my peers and the mothers of my peers to decide which long haired men were cool and which were disapproving. At some point, I could only hope someone would tell me where Jesus and the Apostles fit into and should we take their pictures down from the family room walls.

Most of my thought processing seemed to have a certain pattern, including the types of music I would go on to favor over the course of my life. Since I was unable to hear the most of the words being sung I was only gravitated toward certain tunes which was difficult to find after the mid-nineties. Perhaps there was a King Solomon effect on the musicians after most bands started cutting their hair. Except for Bruce Springsteen. Maybe that's why they called

John B Lester

THAT MIND OF OURS

him the Boss and not the King. Perhaps it was because his band lived on E street. Or it was that he was an artist who just played for the love of reciting music and not the glamour.

A few years later I watched our family slowly discredit my uncle's name for his "recreational habits". Their concern had turned into years of negativism and hurtful comments. A path that imprisoned him to our family own mobile home park which he still resides today. He would be harbored by his mistakes while never receiving his rightful recognition for his exceptional raw talents. He would wear the red scarlet label as the black sheep of the family that eventually shaped the way my generation of cousins perceived him. Despite all this, I only saw him for his extraordinary and craftsmanship skills. To me, he was far from a black sheep. He was a gifted Carpenter. The harsh insensitivity from my family made me wonder if I was adopted. I never till years later that thought was a greater possibility than I had imagined. A decade and a half later I returned home and sat down with him. He would always refer to me as the Doctor, no matter how many times I corrected him. Unfortunately, the years of anger and negativity harbored him from seeing his gifted talents. Along with his generosity and his

John B Lester

THAT MIND OF OURS

heartful caring traits. I could hope that I would one day find a way to tell him, by showing him. His words of wisdom were not the only words of wisdom that wouldn't become clear to me until later in my life. Sometime around 2014 my hearing was retested. I was given the diagnosis that my hearing lost had increased to 75%. My prognosis predicted it would most likely result into complete deafness in my later years. The audiologist attempted to comfort me by telling me that future technology might one-day help. I replied gracefully that my hearing lost was a gift. "75 percent of what people say is bullshit, so I'm really at a 5% advantage. " Coincidently enough that was the first year I had been able to hear most of the words to my childhood songs with the use of modern ear-plugs. Leading me to question whether those words were embedded in my subconscious and thereby predetermining my destiny Here are just a few lines the Boss and others had for me that went beyond the doubts of coincidence.

My Hometown-Bruce Springsteen.

"I'm 35. I got a boy of my own now."

Indeed, I was 35 when I was gifted with my first child.

Glory Days- Bruce Springsteen

"I hope I don't just sit around here talking about the good old days, but I probably will."

John B Lester

THAT MIND OF OURS

And I am glad I did. Hence this book with many stories from my glory days.

Dancing in the Dark. Bruce Springsteen

"I'm just sitting around here trying to write this book. I need a love with some action".

Indeed I repeat, All you need is love. Some nights more than others. Indeed pun intended.

We Built This City on Rock & Roll- Starship.

The title references my last5 years of living in a town of gifted authors. I am not certain if they all were former stars. Or if they came off a ship from the stars.

My Hometown- Bruce Springsteen.

"Son, take a good look around. This is your hometown."

Although this town may not be my hometown. It very well could have been in a previous lifetime. Although my time here has given me an oddly sense of feeling at Home.

My transition into public school began at the start of 7th grade until my senior year graduating class of 550. Those were the years I preferred not to remember. It was period I went through without any

John B Lester

THAT MIND OF OURS

siblings, without any neighborhood friends, without any teammates to call my own. A time when I wasn't athletic enough for team sports, nor studious enough for the academic team. A time when I found myself without any knowledge about fashion or music. I never attended summer camps, nor did I go to any dances. Although my time resided in East Brunswick township, I never knew what a Bar Mitzvah was until I graduated.. Over time I gracefully accepted my fate as the outcast, a school mascot subjected to all levels of bullying from any group. Grades 7 and up became a routine of classes with expectations of daily torment that depended on

John B Lester

THAT MIND OF OURS

which hallway one took. Then one day, the unexpected occurred. It appeared in the form of a curly haired girl with a voice that could carry over any pep rally. "Shut up everyone!" were the words she shouted in my defense. I turned and watched her scold her wide-eyed peers. Later that day she asked about my hearing loss. I squeamishly told her how I mostly lip read their comments. She was fascinated by what she referred to as my "talent" From that day on that group never spoke another demeaning word to me. Or at least any that I could hear. From time to time we made eye contact and exchanged a smile. Sometimes I took an extra

John B Lester

THAT MIND OF OURS

minute to peek in and read her conversations. She often referred to herself as "just an average girl who was everyone's friend". From what I saw, Halley always preferred to listen to what others had to say before taking her turn to speak. And when she spoke, people listened to every word she said. They say the high school years is the time when people find their place. I find that there are those who want people to follow them. And there are those who need someone to follow. Then there are those like Halley who gave people like me hope that I was someone. She was the type of person anyone could hope to be. Halley and I interacted for a total of ten

John B Lester

THAT MIND OF OURS

minutes throughout six years. In that brief time, she gave those years of mine something worth remembering.

John B Lester

THAT MIND OF OURS

The Virgin Tour Ends

My Sophomore-Junior year of high school felt like my second cassette tape album I owned, The Virgin Tour. Being a virgin teenage male, the virgin status was as dreadful as an early century woman with the Scarlet S status. Hell, even a male in his 40's with the virgin status was enough to make a grown man remorse the S syndrome. No one will deny the fact that there is nothing Sexy or Super about a 40-year-old virgin wearing a red S and a cape. Unless that

John B Lester

THAT MIND OF OURS

man's name was Richard Branson. Of course, he was one virgin that could fly high above the clouds without even needing a cape. Reasons, I neglected many of Madonna's songs. Looking back now, I am certain she had a few words of wisdom between the lines of her lyrics. Nevertheless, my teenage years felt as if I would be a virgin forever. Unfortunately for me, the awkward geek persona did not become a trendy group until two decades later when they became known as Fashionably Retro. Fortunately, the extra time I spent at the town's local library gave me one of my life's first rewarding experiences. A meeting between the aisles with my soon to be first

John B Lester

THAT MIND OF OURS

girlfriend. We were immediately drawn together by a common curiosity in French kissing, sex, and everything else that came along with it. Despite our desires to learn more about French kissing, I found it rather ironic we met somewhere along the B aisle while she was researching British time periods. Quite fitting how that same section fell in between books about Birds and Bees. At the time, we were the only couple had that had yet to do "It". Most other couples had already started their love making chapters with multiple notches on their belts with multiple partners under their sheets. Our experience was a bittersweet symphony far from those cheesy

John B Lester

THAT MIND OF OURS

1980's summer camp first time love encounters. Instead, it was an 8-month experimentation mixed with youthful lust and natural curiosity. Eventually we managed to connect our body's apparatuses together, we spent the next six months experimenting each other's body only to fail at making any real chemistry. My first relationship lasted just over a year and 6 months. Although I knew our time had run its course, I still found myself struggling with our separation instead of looking forward to my upcoming summer break. Wondering if I was ever going to have the opportunity to have sex again. Could my mind have been able to listen

John B Lester

THAT MIND OF OURS

to my inner voice at that time I might have realized the library was a haven for those type of potential connections

John B Lester

THAT MIND OF OURS

7th Period Periodic Table

My senior year of high school could have been summed up and broken down into one lesson. A lesson taught by my last period science teacher I referred to as Mister Y. A simple minded man who believed that anything in life worth discussing could be laid out on a table. He was referring to the Periodic Table. A chart of elements responsible for the make up of all living and nonliving things. A lesson that taught me how all people are made from the same basic structure of hydrogen and atoms.

John B Lester

THAT MIND OF OURS

Human beings are different by their unique genetic indemnifiers called DNA. A predetermined code that draws some people to become scientist, and others to become artist. One that gives yields some people with gifted physiques, while making others physically challenged. It is what makes certain people connect as if they always knew each other. While making others clash as if they were oil and water. These are our underlying factors. You might call them our simple factors. Our Y factors. Personality is an entirely different factor. Perhaps the reason people can be so complex. A fitting term you might call the X factor.

John B Lester

THAT MIND OF OURS

In my mind I grew up to believe respect was a determining factor based on ones physique. A preconceived notion that led me into the world of bodybuilding. Being a non-athlete deemed unfit for any of the schools sporting team I reluctantly attended the after school gym, outside the circle of athletes. From time to time I found myself gazing at the display cases of trophies, A hallway of honorable mentions and shiny medallions dedicated to the schools most notable athletes. Known as the Wall of Strength and Courage. A term that coincided with the infamous image of the school's mascot. The Brunswick Golden Bear. It was during those quiet

John B Lester

THAT MIND OF OURS

after school walks down one of the isolated hallways I met another non athlete. A loner type who also hoped to one day earn his name into the hallway of recognition. Perhaps it was a common interest that brought us together. A common bond or a similar make up of hydrogens per say. Either way, he would become my longest lasting friend I referred to as Mister K.

Post-graduation was a time to focus on building a stronger body. Using the basic metals of science, Iron. That summer I spent visiting my father and his new wife in Naples Florida, It was there I upgraded my training to a gold standard. Gold's gym. Even

John B Lester

THAT MIND OF OURS

though it was too late to earn my name into the walls as a Golden Bear. Bodybuilding presented me with a golden opportunity to earn a name for myself.

John B Lester

THAT MIND OF OURS

A Travel Nurses Journey

As far back as I can recall I never desired to save the world. My travels showed me that the world was not in need of saving. My desire was simply to be able to help people. A career choice in travel nursing was my opportunity for me to fill that role. A fast-paced rising profession that crossed the lines of caring with business. It was somewhere along those lines the health care profession lost sight of what they were once aiming for. Travel nursing was more

THAT MIND OF OURS

than just a journey for nurses to see the world. It was an adventure that allowed them to find themselves. A cross country road trip with a chance to learn diverse ways of life. A way to become adaptable to tricky situations while savoring those special occasions. A way to develop the insight of seeing what customs were worth keeping and what traditions were no longer worth continuing. A time I hoped to voice my comparisons with my new place of employment. Unfortunately, it was a time when employers expected travel nurses to be seen working and not heard. Just when the times healthcare was getting closer to unifying. Travel

John B Lester

THAT MIND OF OURS

nurses were being further distanced, as if they were scalawags during a union strike. Denied the rights to feel welcomed. Denied the rights to job security. Denied the right to workplace fairness. That's when my life needed a new journey. Something worth believing in. A purpose worth caring for. A reason to want to help others again. Somewhere along those lines I found someone worth helping. Even when all the odds were against me. I found a way to experience true love. Even if it meant getting nothing in return. I found something worth fighting for. Even when the odds were against them

John B Lester

THAT MIND OF OURS

Crossroads At The Cycle of Sevens

Las Vegas Nevada Dec.31,

It was shortly after midnight during my shift when I looked outside the 8th floor window of my patient's room. The view from the west side of the hospital overlooked the valley of Las Vegas's dessert. "Happy New Year" said a softly spoken voice beside me. Realizing my patient had woken up, I turned and gave her a puzzled looked. "Did you see the fireworks?" she asked "No, I didn't even realize it

John B Lester

THAT MIND OF OURS

was New Year's" I replied. "Well when you get to be my age it's just another day." She then closed her eyes and returned to her peaceful sleep. Quietly pulling the curtains around her bed I thought to myself. "I'm 35 years old and it already seems like just another day. That night I deviated from my routine to update my annual to do list, thirty-eight minutes later and I was still staring at a blank 8x10 white page I titled Resolutions. I had traveled to 5 continents, 21 countries, 38 US states. Somehow, I felt like a lonely gamer playing in a downtown casino keno lounge at 3am realizing he just completed his full card keno for the jackpot.

John B Lester

THAT MIND OF OURS

Deprived of his moment of glory that would permit him to run around the casino grinning like a gritty teenage boy going on his first date. Denied the rights of retelling his winning story repeatedly to his nearby envious gamers while being seduced with cheesy comps from casino host. The game that no one ever plans on winning was over. To me, my adventure book had come to an end as an outline of accomplishments achieved, without having a real story worth telling.

John B Lester

THAT MIND OF OURS

Vegas Juice & Lady Justice

The term "Juice" is refers to the advantage that any gaming casino has over a player. Allow me to simplify the difference between advantage and odds in Vegas terms. A simple wager at the sports desk for team A to win over team B. Without needing to go into point spread. A 100.00 bet wins you 90.00. Risking 100 to win 90. The odds of one tam winning over another is still 50-50. The house edge "Juice" is 10%. Statically the sportsbook over any given

John B Lester

THAT MIND OF OURS

time will produce 10% revenue of all total bets place. No skill. No special system. Just exchanging money.

The roulette wheel has 38 possible numbers. If your number comes in a one-dollar bet wins you 35 dollars. Mathematically if someone places 1 dollar on one set number every spin, that number should come in on the average of every 38 spins. over the lifespan of this wheel spinning almost 24 hours a day. Yet you will only win 35 dollars. The three dollar difference is the house edge or juice. Now that's where the odds become increasingly unfavorable for the player. The slot machines however, are based on a payback system. Meaning one type of

John B Lester

THAT MIND OF OURS

machine may be set to payout 95%. Therefore, it must pay out 950 for every 1000 it takes in. Giving the house their 5% Juice. Over the course of the machines lifetime it will reconfiguration throughout different machines to distribute that 95%. The odds of sitting down and playing the one machine that has taken in 100000000 and has finally configurated to payout its 95% in a 950,000,000-lump sum. Those odds have been calculated by many MIT math overachievers. This merely points out how the casinos make their net profits by maintaining small yet constant advantages in their favor.

John B Lester

THAT MIND OF OURS

Now let's say one of those MIT math geeks you here about playing blackjack sit at a table. If he or she incorporates a way to increase their edge that is called cheating by the casinos. To me that is the oddest of all. If, and only if most players "gain an edge" it merely puts them on par from the disadvantage they started with. At best, they may be able to play with a 5% edge on the house. And 5% doesn't guarantee any player money in the long run unless he can do it 24 hours a day the first time I saw OJ Simpson was in the movie Naked Gun. Since I was not a football fan I did not realize who he was until the day of the infamous white SUV car

John B Lester

THAT MIND OF OURS

chase in 1993. Followed by the trial of the century of course. The first time I met OJ was in New Jersey just after year 2000. The time after that was in Palm Beach Florida in 2007 when we sat next to one another in a gentleman's club. Then shortly afterwards in a nearby steakhouse in Palm Beach which we shared some time. Three years later I was charged with my first offense in Las Vegas NV for being one of the players who found an edge against the house. I would have to go through a series of court dates that lasted nearly a year. During all that time, I sat a row behind or in front of The Juice himself. He would be the only familiar face that sat

John B Lester

THAT MIND OF OURS

near me during the lengthy Clark county judicial process. Makes you wonder what the odds were of that happening?

Extremely unlikely would be my answer then. Well it just happens to take place in the one city where you can bet on anything, you can get an answer for that. Depending on who you ask. Ask any bookie who make their living making bets based on odds and he will tell you a reasonable bet. One that will allow him the edge. Ask any gambler who lives their lives on chances and he will tell you anything's possible. If you were to ask me today I would tell you. Unlikely, but chances are I can get you the correct answer

John B Lester

THAT MIND OF OURS

since I will most likely run into that geeky MIT math genius. At this point of the story you may recognize a familiar theme. The Viva Las Vegas theme. The City of Sin. The new entertainment capital of America. Taking risk for wins. Knowing the odds are always slightly unfavorable. Hoping to hit the big jackpot. Knowing the odds are so unlikely to hit you are more likely to end up in a courtroom with OJ Simpson. Is there any logic in gambling when one is destined to lose? Is there any reason to read a story that is destined to end the same way? Take it from me, there is no logic behind it, but you can bet your ass it's fun. That's all the reason anyone really

THAT MIND OF OURS

needs, otherwise we all be sitting around in libraries reading logics and probabilities trying to figure the odds of being in a Vegas courtroom with OJ Simpson. As cliché as this may sound, I could write a book filled with gambling lifestyle memoirs. Ironically for book writing purposes it would probably be a safe bet. I may very well do so another time now. Just revisiting some of the memories have gotten my old Vegas juices flowing. Here's something to ponder. The house always has the edge therefore the house always wins. The only way to win is to be able to walk away ahead. Every gambler has a story. Every gambler has assorted

John B Lester

THAT MIND OF OURS

reasons behind the gamble. Yet each one will tell you it has nothing to do with money. It that sense how can any gambler ever walk away ahead if they never see themselves as being ahead.

Lastly, while keeping the Vegas juices in mind. My taste for chasing Lady Luck eventually got me a date with Lady Justice. My risk was small enough for me to justify. A first-time offense. I saw this as a never experience to check off my list. Perhaps a story I might be able to laugh about later. I was prepared to pay my fine. The temperature that day was already in the upper ninnies well before 900am. The

John B Lester

THAT MIND OF OURS

courthouse entrance was lined with people. My only wish was to be done before lunchtime in time for me to place my sports bet before their early start time. The Yankees were rivaling the Red Sox that week. And John Lester just happened to be the starting pitcher that day. As I walked down the last corridor before the courtroom I was surprised to see a familiar face walking beside me. It was OJ Simpson. His status was irrelevant to me. I recall our two previous encounters and remember how enjoyable his conversations were. Only a few times during my life was someone able to leave a lasting impression just from a short talk. His laugh more genuine and

John B Lester

THAT MIND OF OURS

sincere than most people I meet on a daily basic. I remember thinking to myself that our day should certainly run smooth now that I had advantage of the juice on my side. Only this time OJ did seem himself. Neither one of our cases went smoothly. My case turned into a never-ending nightmare that lasted into the following year. It didn't matter what my chances were or what edge I thought I had. That would become one lost I paid dearly for and dam just about exiled from the city.

I grew up not following football. Nor do I recall much of OJ's acting career. His name got my attention the

John B Lester

THAT MIND OF OURS

same day most American watched the high-speed chase being filmed SUV spa long the California highways. The trial of the century. From time to time I saw him sitting in that courtroom. The details of the case did not interest me, I formed my thoughts just like everyone else and kept them to myself. They remained the same after the verdict. Then fate allowed us to meet. It wasn't the first time I could feel how someone felt. It was however the first time I found myself seeing what no one else did. The all-American icon with a special personality that brought laughter on the weekly movie. Entertained viewers on the late-night shows. And even gave all

John B Lester

THAT MIND OF OURS

the Sunday fans something to cheer for on Sunday football. That all changed on the one day we all can still remember. The court system gave him a fair trial in front of a jury of his peers. The rest of American reached their own verdict before the trial ever began. That year on trial was more punishment than most people could ever bare to handle. By time his verdict announced him innocent his loyal fans had already turned the most well-known name in pop culture in a savage killer. Slander by those who once loved. Ridiculed by those who never knew him. Tormented by repetitious questions already asked of him.

John B Lester

THAT MIND OF OURS

Whether the life of the woman he loved ended in his hands or by the hands of someone else. The suffering he endured was undoubtable unimaginable. A punishment justified for a crime even if the verdict proves his innocence. Yet very few were convinced of his true innocence. Perhaps too much for anyone to accept. Of all the possibilities for the world to consider no one ever thought to ask the one question of how it felt to be OJ. And if there is one thing I believe OJ and I would agree on. It's that having one person in this world who truly understands you far outweighs the opinion of everyone else in the world.

John B Lester

THAT MIND OF OURS

A Miracle In Sin City

There was this one night while dining sole at 2:00am inside the Suncoast Casino café in Las Vegas Nevada I recall finding myself at that barren crossroad between changing careers and redefining goals. My seven years as a travel nurse allowed me to practice nursing in 20 major hospitals throughout seven states and 12 cities. Each experience was like being thrown into a battlefield to help a staff of weary nurses fighting fatigue from 12 hours of med passing and charting. Reassessing their patients feeling at the bedside had become reprioritize with reorganizing their documentations at the desk side. What was once a caring profession had been replaced by teams of health professionals with no time for caring. I pondered if it was time for me to trade my stethoscope and travel nursing for a deck of cards and travel the World Poker Tour. The next Las Vegas minute shifted my attention toward a young man frantically pleading the casino's security officer to help his friend who had apparently lost conscious while eating. My attempt to get a closer view was blocked by the scolding officer who

John B Lester

THAT MIND OF OURS

dismissed the unconscious victim as another late-night gamer who overindulged on too many comped well drinks. I was already close enough to see the body of another young man who resembles a high school quarterback laying on the floor, his face was lifeless and cyanotic as a frozen corpse. I would spend the next Fourteen minutes breathing respirations into his lungs followed by chest compressions and 3 sets of defibrillated shocks from the portable ADO before I saw the first glimpse of life from his eyes as he struggled to regain conscious. It was just enough to leave me with some hope that this man's life would not end on the floor

John B Lester

THAT MIND OF OURS

of a Las Vegas casino. The following night I arrived for my shift the ER was buzzing with excitement as the day staff reported the events of the young teenager who arrived unresponsive in the middle of the night had just awoken and was in stable condition. It was reported that he was saved by an unknown bystander in the casino who gave him CPR. Once I had come to the surreal terms that young man was the one I had encountered the night before I was left speechless with a mixture of emotions I wasn't familiar with enough to comprehend. The one familiar feeling I was pleasantly surprised to feel was the passion I had

John B Lester

THAT MIND OF OURS

once felt for nursing that came with the rewarding experience of making a difference in someone's life. Although at that time I felt that a career in nursing was not worth fighting over. I always believed that finding a way to make a difference in people's lives was something worth fighting for.

BROKEN HEART IN TEXAS

"Texas" Bullet Formatted

- 1669 miles to Houston. 56 dollars in our wallet. 99 dollars remaining on a gift card. A 7-day old baby. A 3-month-old puppy. Time to trade my playing cards for a cowboy hat.
- Somewhere in Arizona. No gas. Decision to run 3 miles in 110-degree heat or wait 3 hours with no cool air for Triple A. A race against time would trigger my "first" Spartan

John B Lester

THAT MIND OF OURS

race. The hotter it got was only a reminder how hot it will soon be for my family of 3 awaiting my return. Mile 1. A sandstorm. Mile 2. 2min thundershower. Mile 3. A 25-foot fence separating me from the nearest gas station and my finish line.

- Kingwood TX- Home not so sweet home. Postpartum bad days go from bad to worst.
- No resources as the only two responses were:" It's all physiological" and" It's only in your imagination."
- 60 days. 3 county fairs. 6 Asian buffet brunches. And 1 deep fried milky way bar.

THAT MIND OF OURS

- I was told. "You have a new family. A beautiful daughter. And some new in laws. What else can you ask for?" My response. "I could use a friend."
- Ask and you shall receive. AOL chat finds someone online who wants to show me the Houston ropes.
- Would this be a beginning to good story? Or the start of a bad Texas Chainsaw Massacre movie?
- "My name is Brett. I was half asleep when I invited you. I have nothing. I'm anxious. And did I mention I'm on house arrest."

John B Lester

THAT MIND OF OURS

- My comforting answer to a most uncomfortable greeting. "Seems we share a Jail-bond. Your house arrest is by law. Living with my brother in law feels like a house arrest."
- And just like that. A few good laughs, two big smiles, and one new friend.
- Networking within a colorful crowd while working on a Halloween date night.
- A turnout with one off the wagon clergyman. One functional incoherent Irishman. And one black street trickster. All inside a three story, twelve room haunted mansion with no

electricity. Without any formal residents. With no knowledge of how many ghost or goblins may be residing.

- Would this night with a trio from the rainbow club be my chance to strike gold and impress the girl or would it just be wishful thinking?
- No matter if it was haunted house or Texas roadhouses. Creepy crowd or scary carnival rides. The girl just wasn't into me.
- Then I swore I heard a creepy voice saying, "Careful what you wish for."

John B Lester

THAT MIND OF OURS

- Although it wouldn't be until sometime much later. That night would eventually become one hell of a story to tell.
- The night in the mystery house had a mysterious way of working out.

John B Lester

THAT MIND OF OURS

The Calling

It was time for my 2:00 am break. Once again, I found myself sitting at another dark nurse's station staring down at a blank paper. I thought to myself, "Is this what I risked everything for? My story couldn't possible end here. Could it?" My thoughts drifted as I stared into the neon blue aquarium glowing from the patient waiting room across the hallway. Suddenly my phone vibrated as an unknown number appeared in my incoming call

John B Lester

THAT MIND OF OURS

window. Uncertain of who might be calling me at that hour, I answered with a slight hesitation in my voice. "Hello. I'm not sure who's number this is. I saw your number on a call list from Brett's phone. I'm sorry to inform you. He has passed away last night. If you are interested in service arrangements, you may call me tomorrow. My name is Jim.

The following week Jim had returned my call pass the date of Brett's services. We spoke for a while. The comfort that comes with having an easy two-way conversation was mutual. Neither dared to ask either one anything personal as it might be the last

John B Lester

THAT MIND OF OURS

words. The invitation was offered to meet at a local dog park. "How is your day?" he asked, "Considering the only friend I met here so far has passed away, I suppose it is somewhere between sub-par and fair at best." I replied. Jim lived in a two-bedroom apartment with his son who was slightly younger than me. The living room was surrounded by an abundance of miscellaneous items neatly piled that left little space to walk around. It would be incorrect to call him a hoarder or even messy, as I sensed that each item had its very own special story. I sat down on a rolling chair seated in front of a faded checkerboard. Jim took out a sealed yellow

John B Lester

THAT MIND OF OURS

envelope the size of a business card and slid it across the board before sitting onto a small stool across from me. "Oh, I had forgotten about that." I said. Jim placed his hand on his chin and began humming to himself while intermittently peeking over at the channel 9 news. "You play chess Jim? Now that is a thinker's game. A game in which the players study each other more than the board. Would you agree?" Jim gave me a big agreeing node. "Are we still getting to know one another, or have we entered the profiling point?" Jim looked up at me and mildly asked "Does that make you uncomfortable?" I looked back at him and grinned.

THAT MIND OF OURS

"Not at all. I'm a poker man myself. Texas hold 'em. Only I never actually played in Texas." I had already mentally prepared myself as if I was about to be all in. "I don't take you for much of a gambling man. Am I correct?" I questioned. Jim remained stoic and attentive. "Your correct. I played some keno slots back when I was working in Japan. I'll have to tell you that story some time. That time I was eating Kobe beef almost every night." I laughed. It was sometimes difficult to remain on one topic when we could talk about anything for hours on end.

"You would be surprised on how differently people respond when something is at risk. For example, we

John B Lester

THAT MIND OF OURS

could flip a coin for the envelope. Winner takes all." I explained. Jim thought for a moment before replying. "We could do that. Then what fun is that if we might not get to play another hand?"

My eyes lit up as if his answer was precisely the card I hoped he would throw out. "My thoughts exactly Jim. Who would want any story with so much potential to end. Especially since we are just getting to know one another." Jim adjusted his position. "If you have time I would love to show you some of my family pictures I recently found. My mom never threw any of them away." I accepted his offer. "You said you moved here from where?' Jim turned around and recited his previous 15-year timeline exactly as he told me twice before, without missing a syllable out of place. "Jim. If I may guess. You come from a science background?" He nodded yes, and proceeded to tell me about his former position he held at U.S. Steel. Jim was centering a few checker pieces carefully within their square box. Then he stretched his finger two rows over and tapped on the envelope. "Don't forget that before you leave." He said nonchalantly." Jim lifted his eyes and awaited my next move. I took another look around the musty, smoke filled room and muttered

John B Lester

THAT MIND OF OURS

under my breath. "Those guys in Vegas will never know what it's like to play real poker, until they have played poker deep in the heart of Texas."

"I'm going to make a proposal to you. If my read is as sharp as it's been known for. I take the prize package home. If my read is off. Then I stand here before you knowing I guessed wrong." I declared.

Jim took a step back and slightly lowered his head before agreeing. "You're an honorable man. A loyal man. To his company. His work. His cause. Your worked left little time for love. Which is why the pictures remain in their boxes instead of on your

John B Lester

THAT MIND OF OURS

walls. Yet you have felt heartache. You believe you can conceal that just by becoming another person. Love is the one formula a man of science can never quite find a simple solution for. The US Steel title fits you well. I sense there would be no better person to take on the job of creating a modern Superman. "With one swift reach I picked up the small envelope and slipped into my pocket. Jim remained motionless as I walked toward the door. "Same time next week Jim? I want to see those pictures." He nodded quickly. I could hear his muffled deep voice respond." Thank you. Call me later John." Jim and I

John B Lester

THAT MIND OF OURS

have been friends ever since the day I answered that call.

John B Lester

THAT MIND OF OURS

Florida Nurse Takes a Stand to Congress

When John Lester first found out he was going to be a first-time father at the age of 35 he knew it was time to find a place his family could settle their roots and call home. Relocating from the sin city of Nevada to the heart of Texas to be with his future in laws seemed like the right thing to do. After a year of establishing himself while working for a Houston hospital as a specialty RN he made the decision to

John B Lester

THAT MIND OF OURS

further his education with a Master's degree. He confided with is family physician about his difficulty maintaining focus with studies and his trouble sleeping. He was referred to a specialist who diagnosed him with ADHD and insomnia and began treating him with prescribed medication. A brief time later his employer selected him for random hospital drug screening. Two weeks later his place of employment notified him of a positive result and his immediate termination. He informed the hospital administration as well as the Texas Board of Nursing of his prescribed medications. With no support from any of his resources and little finances

John B Lester

THAT MIND OF OURS

left to seek out costly attorneys he knew his options were running out quickly. A month later he received a job offer from a hospital in southwest Florida and without hesitation he and his family headed for the sunshine state leaving his traumatic experiences in Texas behind him. Little did he know that the worst part of his Texas experience was yet to come. From December 2012 until May of 2015 he and his family enjoyed being part of their local Charlotte County community. While working for a hospital in Port Charlotte Mr. Lester became involved as a member Florida's union for nurses. Having previously worked as a travel nurse for ten years he had grown

John B Lester

THAT MIND OF OURS

accustomed to working under contracts with no job security or job protection. He believed having an organization protecting the nursing community was not just a key to improving nurses working conditions, it was the key to improving the entire healthcare system.

In June 2015, John was offered a nursing position with a substantial increase in pay and benefits by another hospital. Before he could respond with a decision he was informed by the potential employer that his nursing license had been suspended. John promptly inquired with the Florida

Board of Nursing and was directed to an assigned compliance officer. The compliance officer was not able to disclose the reason for his suspension. Additionally, he informed John that he was unable to speak to any members of the board about the details of the suspension or request reinstatement until he received approval to appear in front of the board's meeting which was held every other month. The request would not be considered until he completed requirements. Upon obtaining a copy of the final order from the Board of Nursing it stated that they were unable to reach Mr. Lester and thereby elected to file a complaint for violation of

John B Lester

THAT MIND OF OURS

Florida Statue 464.018b(b)-Having a license to practice nursing revoked, suspended, or otherwise acted against, including the denial of licensure, by the licensing authority of another state, territory, or country.

He was denied the right to work and suffered lost wages for a period of 12 months. Which violates the 8th amendment and his Constitutional rights. It also violated the 6th amendment rights to a speedy trial/hearing within reasonable time. Lester was continually told by IPN he had to comply with all IPN requirements to be granted a hearing in front of the board. In February 2016 Mr. Lester was still waiting for his hearing. Using the last of his retirement savings to support his family while continuing to pay IPN excessive fees costing over $ 3,000 he was then told he had to sign a formal contract agreeing to continue the program or he would be denied his hearing for reinstatement. On April 6th Mr. Lester appeared in front of the board with documentation proving he had prescriptions for his positive drug screening in Texas dated back in 2012. He also stated Texas never notified him they would be suspending his license, nor would he have any reason to believe they would since he reported his prescriptions to them following his termination. The Board responded to Mr. Lester's official public hearing statement by saying his license suspension had nothing to do with anything that happened in Texas. When Mr. Lester's attorney requested his removal from the IPN he was denied and told to complete one year of IPN just for being on a prescription medication. On April 27th his license was reinstated. However, his license status was posted on their public website as Active with Obligations. Since the term obligations is not clearly stated anywhere on their website or the nursing practice act Mr. Lester has been denied

THAT MIND OF OURS

employment from two potential employers for reasons directly related to this undefined status. Mr. Lester is currently seeking the assistance from his State's Senator and will continue to present his case to members of the Senate and the public until the necessary changes are made to these governing state agencies. Changes that holds state agencies accountable for unjust, excessive, and inhumane punishment given to anyone discriminated against based on assumptions of addiction or mental illness. Mr. Lester was recently asked "After everything you have been through, is it still worth fighting for just for a license?" Mr. Lester responded." Of course not, no

John B Lester

THAT MIND OF OURS

license is worth that kind of a fight. But a chance to make a difference that's helps so many others. Even if it is a small chance, now that's worth fighting for."

John B Lester

THAT MIND OF OURS

It was 2 years and 9 months ago when being a writer was still just a dream of mine. A fantasy that rejuvenated itself just before any trip down to Key West, home of the infamous Ernest Hemmingway. This trip was on Halloween Eve. Just in time to catch the final two days of Fantasy Fest 2015.That early morning I awoke from a vivid dream that was as pixel clear as a movie from Disney's studios. Being aware that most dreams are forgotten after the first awaken minute, I jumped out of bed and scribbled a few notes to remind me. I felt certain this dream was so unique that it was meant to be my first story. After 2 fantastic days of festivities the images of my

John B Lester

THAT MIND OF OURS

dreams were still flickering between my thoughts and sub conscious. When I returned the paper had vanished. After an hour of scavenging my daughter spoke "Sometimes dreams just become lost."

A week later, during the middle of a sleepless night, I wrote down my first short story. It would result in the completion of my first short story. Shortly afterwards, an emerging investment company by the name of Prosper announced my story as the top entry for their holiday contest. It was the first time in all my years of writing I was given a sense of validation from those around me. It became the driving force of inspiration that made me believe this story was one worth sharing. With help from a team of illustrators from India, our story was published in my first book titled, The Story of Team Prosper.

John B Lester

THAT MIND OF OURS

John B Lester

THAT MIND OF OURS

John B Lester

THAT MIND OF OURS

The Making of a Town Book

With that noted I signed up for my first Writers workshop hosted by Chuck S. whose credentials included several publications including one which was produced into a movie directed by Robert Zemeckis. His workshop tour was scheduled throughout the major US cities. It also presented a chance for authors to Pitch their query letter to various agents from major publishing houses.

John B Lester

THAT MIND OF OURS

From a marketing perspective I saw no reason to believe readers would be interested in what an unknown writer had to say. However, I did believe in the power of words. And as always, I believed in the value of a good story. Since my timeline as a writer had just started my only thought was to start from the bottom. I remember thinking "Nothing to fear, so much to say, with nowhere to start." Then my voice of reason whispered . "You don't need to be a king to be a good writer." Although not the best choice of words in the writing world. They were words of encouragement in my mind. Come to think of it, I wasn't aware of how any well-known writer started.

John B Lester

THAT MIND OF OURS

I only knew of two reporters that got their start doing newspaper reviews. Following the footsteps of Clark Kent and Peter Parker I walked into the local newspaper. It was the beginning of the week, a new day in the middle of summer. Having time on my hand seemed like the time to try a new career. That good energy and some luck I finagled my way into an interview with their busy editor. The gray-haired man named John compelled a spitting image of how anyone might vision a newspaper editor. In between our small talk I admitted to having no prior writing experience. I denied having completed any writing courses. Then stated how I was never one to read

John B Lester

THAT MIND OF OURS

newspapers at all. At that point I didn't think my 24-page picture book would win the interview. In fact, I wondered if I might need to work my way up to the bottom. My offer to work as an intern was left on the table and proceeded to brain storm my next plan of action. The idea to write a town book would be a way to collaborate local networking while trialing the road to self-publication. A few in.   A few months of late weekend nights of Google researching I needed to test the waters to plan accordingly. With only one 8x5 24-page holiday picture book I saw this as trial and error quest to test the non-internet markets for potential books in the future books. As it turns out

John B Lester

THAT MIND OF OURS

the community was very encouraging and eager to help new authors. My first few doors to door calls landed me two book signing offers for the upcoming season. A fantastic opportunity for exposure for any author using the power of words of mouth. A marketing benefit far more valuable than the handful of units sold. A key factor most retailers looked for was someone with multiple items or maskable merchandise to supplement their product. It was unlikely I would have another book by then, but it gave me time to seek out plush toys, coloring activity books and even clothing with the characters images on them. Information well worth a few trips to the local book stores. During that time I spent creating flyers, brochures, business cards. I even went through the process of applying for all the steps of opening a business to be my own distributor. Each step was repeated so that I was fully prepared and license for a catering business. A business I saw as the opportunity for my wife to experience the same joy in doing what she loved. A common bond in the business aspect. After a summer of encouragement from our family and friends she had shown she agreed to try the venture. It was many afterthoughts later I versioned another marketing opportunity by promoting my book as her marketing merchandise.

John B Lester

THAT MIND OF OURS

The following week I made an appointment with the Chamber of Commerce to participate in our towns upcoming summer events. Officially establishing Mahals Kitchen.

The town book planning led to my first web writing. Writing local reviews for a trendy website called Trip Advisor. A great to kill two birds in one stone. Considering the site's infamous owl logo that might be the best choice of words. Let's just say I found a site that took me under its wing. By the summer ends each of my reviews came with their own personalized story. By the summers end I covered most of the towns highlights and some of their hidden treasures. After 55 reviews I was titled Areas Top Reviewer. Perhaps the owl's way of saying I was ready to spread my wings as a writer

Using that philosophy, I put the brainstorming into motion. I wanted to write something for everyone. An adventure for the family to read. Something that taught history, science. Hence making this the point on my timeline to attempt my first novel.

John B Lester

THAT MIND OF OURS

The Invitation

My time writing local reviews I found other means of book promoting. Adult centers, libraries, farmers markets. Even local book stores willing to promote theme parties around my book's theme. Now all I needed was to write a book. Nonetheless, this quest led to another means that became quite meaningful. The book store's monthly author signing would lead to an invitation to the town's writers group. It would be the first time I had a group to call my own. A group that enjoyed sharing their stories and poetry. My appreciation was more than words could say.

John B Lester

THAT MIND OF OURS

That is when I decided to write them a poem of my own.

John B Lester

THAT MIND OF OURS

WHEN DID A SOCIAL FACE TO FACE CHAT REQUIRE A CERTAIN SKILL?

MY NEWEST I-PHONE GADGET HAS TOO MANY WIDGETS AND NOT ENOUGH SPACE

CAN'T CHECK MY LATEST G MAILS. FORGETTING THE PASSWORDS IS SADLY THE CASE

MY OLD LAPTOP FAR TOO SLOW FOR MY NETFLIX DOWNLOADS

John B Lester

THAT MIND OF OURS

CAN'T REMEMBER WHERE I PUT MY KINDLE TO STREAM MY UPLOADS

CONSTANT PICTURES APPEAR ON MY FACEBOOK TIMELINE

ENDLESS EMAILS FROM EVERYONE'S FRIENDS, BUT NONE FROM MINE

A SIMPLE CONVERSATION AND FLAVORED TEA IS SOMETHING I WISH FOR

A TWO WAY TALK NO

John B Lester

THAT MIND OF OURS

COMPLICATIONS, A FEW LAUGHS, AND MAYBE SOME ADDED SPICE, NOTHING MORE

THERE I MET THREE WRITERS, THE THIRD I BARELY HAD A CHANCE TO GREET

YET HE TOOK THE TIME TO LEAVE ME A MESSAGE ABOUT A GROUP HE THOUGHT I SHOULD MEET

"COME TO THE LIBRARY ON THE

SECOND FLOOR, THE THIRD TUESDAY OF THE MONTH, JUST SHORTLY AFTER LUNCH"

SO, I MADE A MENTAL NOTE AND STARTED THINKING, "THIS COULD BE AN INTERESTING BUNCH."

WITH NO EXPECTATIONS, NO PREPARATION, NO BOOK IN HAND, I ARRIVED WONDERING IF I WAS INVADING THEIR SPACE

John B Lester

THAT MIND OF OURS

SUDDENLY A PLEASANT VOICE SPOKE "WE HAVE A NEW FACE HERE AND WE COULDN'T BE MORE DELIGHTED" THAT'S WHEN I KNEW I COME TO THE RIGHT PLACE

THIS GROUP OF FIFTEEN SHARED THEIR LOVE FOR STORIES, AND THEY EACH HAD SEVERAL TO TELL

FROM DIFFERENT POINTS IN TIME, THEY ALL MADE IT A POINT TO

John B Lester

THAT MIND OF OURS

RHYME, AND EVERYONE TOLD THEM SO VERY WELL

THERE WAS A DISTANT MAN WHO SAT SO VERY STILL, ABRAHAM WAS HIS NAME

HIS POWERFUL VOICE TRAVELED FAR, IT WAS QUITE MOVING TO HEAR, AS VERY FEW COULD DO THE SAME

THEN BONNIE SPOKE OF HER AGE AND WHITE HAIR WITH ELEGANCE

John B Lester

THAT MIND OF OURS

AND GRACE

SHE THEN PROUDLY ANNOUNCED HER WEB ADDRESS ENTITLED WHITE SPACE

ONE LADY EMPOWERED HER WORDS DEMANDING ALL WOMEN BE PAID EQUALLY BECAUSE THAT'S THE WAY IT SHOULD BE

I DIDN'T HAVE THE HEART TO TELL HER THAT BATTLE WAS ALREADY

THAT MIND OF OURS

WON BACK IN 1963

HER BOLD STATEMENT SPOKEN FROM HER FEARLESS HEART, EVERYONE PROUDLY LISTENED TO EVERY WORD SHE HAD TO SAY

KNOWING THAT VOICES LIKE HERS EARNED WOMEN THE EQUAL RIGHTS THEY HAVE TODAY

THE CORNER CHAIR BELONGED TO CHARLES FROM MANCHESTER

John B Lester

THAT MIND OF OURS

"REAL ENGLISHMAN WRITE POETRY AND DRINK TEA"

"SO, IF YOU DO SO TOO, THEN MATES WE MAY BE"

"WOULD YOU BELIEVE, HE INVITED ME, FOR THAT CUP OF TEA?"

A LOVELY WRITER TO MY RIGHT PAINTED VIVID COLORS ALL AROUND HER FRONT DOOR

RED DOOR, BLUE DOOR, BROWN DOOR

John B Lester

THAT MIND OF OURS

AND MORE, EACH ONE BRIGHTER THAN THE ONE BEFORE

ASKING HER WHY SHE PAINTED THEM, SO MANY COLORS WOULD SEEM UNFAIR

CONSIDERING SHE WOULD NOT HAVE SUCH A REMARKABLE STORY TO SHARE

GLANCING TO MY LEFT DANIEL AND BABS WROTE EROTIC ROMANCES

John B Lester

THAT MIND OF OURS

FROM WHAT I COULD SEE

WHISPERING TO THEM I INQUIRED "DO YOU HAVE ROOM FOR ONE MORE, TO MAKE IT THREE?"

"WOULD YOU BELIEVE, THEY INVITED ME, FOR THAT CUP OF TEA?

John B Lester

THAT MIND OF OURS

After my review of the Military Heritage Museum, I thought, another picture book would be a fun project for the local vets to enjoy. The title would be Turing Turtle's First Day at Eagles Academy. As I may have mentioned before, the best part of a storybook is the story behind the book. Now this is where things start getting real interesting. This book was completed during the final week of summer. The evening our family would be attending my daughter's open house session for her upcoming start of the 6th grade. Our family agreed this was reason for a pre-dinner celebration. A chance for me to review one of the downtown hot spots we had not yet dined at. It

John B Lester

THAT MIND OF OURS

was a fitting way to kill three turtles in one stone. To our surprise our place of choice was called Turtles Cove. Afterwards we arrived at her new soon to be school. This was the shell shocker.

Eagles Middle School.

John B Lester

THAT MIND OF OURS

John B Lester

THAT MIND OF OURS

"Class, I want to welcome Turing Turtle to our class," said the Professor. "He is our new transfer student from Hawaii. I would appreciate if everyone would help to make him feel like a part of our class".

After showing Turing to his seat, the Professor finished with his lesson. "That concludes our lesson about the attack on Pearl Harbor and all

John B Lester

THAT MIND OF OURS

of the brave soldiers who fought for our freedom during World War II."

The Professor notices Turing not paying attention. "Excuse me Mr. Turtle, would you care to join us? Why aren't you paying attention?"

Turing slowly turned his head toward his teacher. While looking through the thick lenses of his black glasses, he sees the rest of the class

John B Lester

THAT MIND OF OURS

snickering at him. "I'm very sorry sir, I didn't hear you," he said.

"Daydreaming on your first day? Well, it seems you do not need to listen since you must know enough about today's lesson. Why don't you stand up and share your thoughts with the rest of the class?" The Professor stood in front of the class, hands on hips, waiting for Turing to reply.

John B Lester

THAT MIND OF OURS

The only sound came from one of the class bullies. "Maybe he's just too slow to catch up with us," he sneered.

The class began to snicker and giggle with little regard for their new classmate's feelings.

"Settle down class. We want Turing to tell us what he knows about the war, don't we?", said the Professor.

John B Lester

THAT MIND OF OURS

"My father had a different job during the war," said Turing. "He was an artillery gunner. Turtles were best for this job since they are born deaf. The heavy firing would not distract them, and they could remain focused on their job."

Turing continued, "war was never about defending freedom. War is the reason we lost our freedom."

The Professor looked shocked. "That's quite a statement Mr. Turtle; please continue."

John B Lester

THAT MIND OF OURS

So, Turing continued to explain what he knew about War. "When we are born into this world, we begin with the gift of being pure, or natural. We call that Raw. Naturally, we grow up seeing each new experience as a wondrous treasure. We see the good in everyone we meet. Our basic emotions are filled with love and trust. Turtles believe that when those natural, raw emotions are turned around long enough, Raw becomes War."

One of the children who had been making fun of Turing asked him, "what do you mean?"

John B Lester

THAT MIND OF OURS

Turing was happy to answer, "war results from those who have allowed their natural emotions to become filled with anger. The anger brings destruction to all those surrounding them, especially anyone who sees things differently than they do."

Turing spoke to the children who had laughed at him earlier. "My father shared lots of stories with me. He spoke about times when our ancestors were known as dinosaurs and roamed our planet in peace."

The classroom grew noisy with excitement. "You're part of the dinosaur family? Tell us more stories about your family!"

The Professor stood in front of the class as his new student, Turing Turtle, shared stories of the war, Hawaii, and his Dinosaur ancestors, with the rest of the class.

John B Lester

THAT MIND OF OURS

The Professor asked, "Turing, do you mean to tell me that turtles cannot hear at all? Why didn't you tell anyone?"

"Well," answered Turing, "no one ever asked me. Everyone just assumed I wasn't paying attention."

John B Lester

THAT MIND OF OURS

Seventeen months later I had authored 4 books including my first novel. Feeling inspired to begin my 3rd picture book. Just as I got into that writer's rhythm my pen ink began fading. It appeared my fresh new notebooks were made with paper that repelled my special writing pens. Not wanting to lose my inspiration I reached for the old composition book that appeared to be decomposing over time. As I turned the 3rd page I stared down at a cluster of barely legible scribbled words. It was in fact the dream notes I had written the day before my Key

John B Lester

THAT MIND OF OURS

West trip. A most rewarding reminder that Even Lost Dreams Can Be Found.

This story involves a fish that was thought to be a beta fish. A fish that grew unique features which resembled an endangered species known as the Razorback Sucker. Their population greatly declined over recent decades and is believed to only exist in parts of the Colorado river. Whether this Razorback Sucker found its way into a little girls fish bowl in Florida. Or this beta fish transformed into the likes of a shark. Both scenarios remain a mystery. People are very much like small fish in a

John B Lester

THAT MIND OF OURS

big pond. We often do not appreciate them or realize how special they are until they are gone.

It was the night before the last day of April, the day that would have been my father's birthday. The evening was free from interruptions, making it feel as if I had all the time required to complete my list of things to do. I sat in my old rolling chair and turned on my outdated laptop, pondering where my next adventure would take me next. The quiet room away from the rest of the household reminded of the empty nurse's station back during my years in Las Vegas. The stiffness in my neck suddenly began to ease as I took a moment to stretch. Glancing down at my old brown FM AM radio clock reminded me of the ones used inside Motel 6 rooms I used to stay at in Edison New Jersey. Surprised to see how early it still was, I began organizing my unfinished paperwork and placed them neatly on my desktop. Before continuing I retrieved a freshly new white 8x10 paper from the printer draw to reprioritize my to do list. Just after writing the

THAT MIND OF OURS

heading entitled To Do at the top of the paper I took a minute to look back at that New Year's Night. The nostalgic moment gave me a tingling sensation down my back brought on by a feeling of wholeness and gratification. I picked up my pen and smiled as I crossed out the words To Do and replaced them with, Resolutions.

1. Begin piano lessons with my oldest daughter, so that we may one day perform our own Dueling Pianos.
2. Buy my youngest daughter her first soccer ball, and watch her accomplish her first goal.
3. Share these stories with some friends. Then Hope that we make a few new stories of our own.
4. Continue traveling the world. This time seeing it with a new perspective. Be a tour guide for family and friends and see the world through their eyes.

John B Lester

THAT MIND OF OURS

After months of sending queries, personal emails, tweets, there was no response to my first novel. Nevertheless, as with all my life's adventures I never feared failure nor was I afraid to make mistakes. And I always believed no harm could come from a good trial. Unless you happen to be OJ Simpson. Fortunately, my trial showed me there was a high demand for human connection. It seemed I didn't need to write a best-selling novel to write a biography. Although readers may not have shown interest in my novel, people sure seemed interested in what I had to say. Perhaps this was interpreted this form of redirection rather than rejection. Perhaps it was only in my mind. Either way I began reformatting a few blogs some old notes from my previous story titled That Mind of Mine. By using a new

THAT MIND OF OURS

voice, I eventually turned them into a book stories behind my storybooks. This time using a more fitting title. **That Mind of Ours.**

John B Lester

THAT MIND OF OURS

The Voice and The Mind

My Voice: I suppose it's seems just as fitting to use the term Old Soul when referring to me. Nevertheless, I never thought this type of communication was possible. And now that we are here together, I am still fathomed that it would be I who has much questions to ask of you. I suppose we can discuss most of them in due time. For the good gesture of our story it would be most timely to begin from our beginning. Tell me. Do you recall our first encounter?

My Mind: Indeed, I do. You probably know that was a day I have never forgotten. The details of day remain more vivid than any other memory during that time of my life. The time I climbed the pine tree. 6th grade. Robert and Elaina made it look like an easy jump onto the school's rooftop. I remember being so fearful. I think I was fearful of just about everything back then. Almost made it. Probably would succeeded if I hadn't been so afraid. How long was I hanging on that rooftop? Seems like it was eternal even looking back at it now. Then the fall. That long downward fall seemed so peaceful. The only time during that day I wasn't scared. And how can I forget that ever so soft landing. Till this day I can still remember the feeling of falling onto a pile of feathered pillows. There was no way I should have walked off from that. Landing directly on my back no less. You were there? How? In spirit form? I don't recall any angels with enormous white wings.

That conversation would mark one of our first interactions in first/second person format we were able to write as it occurred in real time. There is more to that dialogue and even more to the story of my Voice and who "She" was and her

John B Lester

THAT MIND OF OURS

previous life. As she said earlier, those stories are for another time. I am happy to report these tales are quite humorous as well as eccentric. Although none of them fascinated me as much as our reminiscences through our timeline together when we interacted as one. Even with everything I have seen and have come to understand, there are still times I find it difficult to distinguish my voice from my own imagination. Nevertheless, of stories during our timeline together are even more difficult to deny the presence of something more than the ordinary. Shortly after the tree falling incident life seemed to become a battle between a developed common sense and a under developed extra sense.

    My Voice. Remember Big Bob?

My Mind: Yes. I would imagine being able to breath in water while swimming to the bottom of our 7-foot pool at that time. My lungs were young, my capacity for air was very limited. That was the day my parents hosted a pool party. Big Bob weighed around 350 pounds, and was enjoying leisure time floating in our pool raft. I was at the bottom of the pool trying to expand my reach to the bottom of the pool. A rather unfortunate day to overestimate my limitations as I ran out of air too soon before surfacing above water. My exit was blocked under the raft occupied by Big Bob. I could hear the echoing in my ears each time my head hit the bottom of the raft as if I was being punched by a school yard bully. I panicked. The water became extremely dark. The next moment I emerged above from the water while turning over Big Bob from the raft.

My Voice: There were many potential dangers in your life. Some of them were more dangerous at the time, others were more damaging over time. The road you

John B Lester

THAT MIND OF OURS

resided on during that pool party was Old Stage Road. Your mind was asked that question a dozen times over the last 3 years and, yet you never recalled it. And yet today you write it as if it were yesterday. Your mind and body were not always gifted. That came in your latter years and continues to progress. Your mind and body has been gifted in the same way as many others before you. It was your heart and soul that gave you uniqueness.

My Mind: It was shortly afterwards from the time of the pool party when another life experience occurred. My daily walk with my dog Jet. Three boys on bikes. At first, no different than any other bully. Then something didn't feel right, a sudden surge of fear overcame me for no reason. They had not done any harm except for typical bullying words, yet somehow, I sensed they were not going to stop there. My ordinarily affectionate dog turned into a growling beast I had never seen before. It took all my strength to restrain him from lunging at the boys. The look of terror on the boys faces as they raced off were as if they had never seen a growling dog before.

My Voice: There were times you needed extra strength and ways to project fear. The time alone with that man when you were an altar boy.

My Mind: In a church, no less. He was extremely aggressive as well as intimidating. The same feeling of impending gloom came about. He placed his hand on my shoulder. When I turned to look at him he had that very same look of terror on his face. He immediately demanded I leave the room. It was as if he heard the voice of God.

John B Lester

THAT MIND OF OURS

My Voice: Or rather he saw the look of something else. There were other times.

My Mind: The big city back alley's we were told never to go into. Over the years I would almost search for those type of places. A way of testing my courage or perhaps a way of testing if those incidents were merely coincidences.

My Voice: Then there was the Tenderloin in San Francisco. One of history books infamous Do Not Enter areas. Only that was a time you showed me something. You did not need to project fear with your strength or other means that day. You got that same Fight or Flight aura from those with harmful intentions. Instead, you proceeded to humor them with your story about your 1:00 am trip to the nearby massage parlor that cheated you. You defused their ill intentions with laughter to the point they were sincerely enjoying your presence. Maybe enough to deviate those ill intentions from the next wondering person passing through those alley's. Your current lifetime are reminders and recurrences of your prior timeline. As well as hints to your life that has yet to come.

John B Lester

THAT MIND OF OURS

Past Stories Reveal The Future

There were some places I seemed to purposely avoid. One of them being the Alcatraz tour in San Francisco. The idea of being imprisoned never appealed to me, no matter how challenging the escape may have been. With that said, there were one other thing I was gravitated toward more than swim time. That was movie time. Mainly being, it was time spent with my father. My parents officially divorced when I was 9. Unofficially divorced years prior to that. My time became limited with Dad. Even then most of our time was overshadowed by his beaten spirits. Those beaten spirits never appeared during our movie time. A time I looked forward to seeing the look of anticipation on his face as we scrolled through

John B Lester

THAT MIND OF OURS

the movie times of the Friday newspaper. A time when I was guaranteed to see his joyful smile. A time when our post movie discussions were like conversations with a best friend..

. Once I truly found my inner voice, writing became like a conversation fueled with someone you love. A fatherly love, a brotherly love, and a love of partnership all at once. And once I truly believed that all one needs is love, I had to wait for the only source of love I had to awaken. It makes any story run as smooth as a well-produced movie. And with that note, let me tell you the story of the two most important movies in my life. The first came about on a Friday evening with Dad. That night I was more excited than usual since Mom had just bought me a red bandana similar to the one members of the E street band wore. Upon Dad's arrival, it was clear his beaten

John B Lester

THAT MIND OF OURS

spirit had gotten the best of him. Just after closing the passenger car door he quickly removed the bandana off my head and began unraveling it. After I questioned him he told me he was inspecting for joints. I sat quietly in the car feeling slightly disappointed. Here I thought that only long hair gave people the assumption of drug usage . This abnormal notion of thinking was unlike my father and most likely came from one of those day time talk shows of useless information. When we arrived at the movie theater we had not spent our usual time determining our movie of choice. Our arrival time of 715 left us with two choices. The popular talked about Rodney Dangerfield titled Back to School or another unknown feature involving time travel. Since school was one of those things I purposely avoided at any cost, it was an obvious choice to see the one titled Back to the Future.The movie's setting portrayed a young man who

John B Lester

THAT MIND OF OURS

was always late for school and his close friend, a crazy doctor with notions about time travel. The film went on to strike me even more on a personal level.. At that time, one might relate this movie to my own story as a meeting of coincidences. Looking back at it thirty years later one might believe differently. In the end, the main character changes history through time travel. As a result, his father became a respected man of confidence who published his own story into a book. He tells his son "You see. You can accomplish anything if you put your MIND into it." And in the end, it was love that saved them both. The love for each other, the love of a girl, and the love of an old wise friend.

The second most important movie I considered to be premiered the spring of 1993. The year of my high school graduation. Just before my journey off to college, my first

John B Lester

THAT MIND OF OURS

time away from home. I realize my story does not mention anything about mothers. My mother and those who have been a mother to me were hard women with rough surfaces. Anyone judging their cover might even portray them as being bitches .Most of my time toward them was spent feeling resentful, neglected, and bitterness toward them. with me. Even with my abilities to read people I never had much desire to read into them. Perhaps the last few years of them minding my business has given them some mindfulness. It was movies that showed me how some women can only show their love behind closed doors. No pun intended. It merely means they act as hidden figures in our lives. I suppose this type of love is tough love that works two ways.. Even as I am writing this book, I cannot be certain this is my case. It's merely my mind being hopeful.

John B Lester

THAT MIND OF OURS

This movie I am referring to is about the life of a simple man who saw the world around him as not being different. Instead he simply saw the world for what it was. His name was Forrest Gump. The beginning of the movie reveals how his mother was forced to raise her child on her own. She refused to have the world judge her son by his outside demeanor just as the world had done to her. Anyone who saw the movie might remember the early scene involving a meeting with the school principal. "My boy may be different, but he will get the same chances as everyone else." It was a true sign of tough love behind closed doors. Then again, she had to accept the principal bribe which concluded the meeting behind the doors of her bedroom. Nevertheless, a sign of tough love. Here are some other notables which made this movie personable to me.

John B Lester

THAT MIND OF OURS

"He would play his music guitar in a way that made me want to move my hips and shake my legs. Some years later they called that man King. It must be hard being a King." A young Forrest Gump referring to a young unknown singer at the time named Elvis Presley. Since the idea of any type of imprisonment was always unappealing to me I was never interested in any music written by any King known for his Jailhouse Rock. However, coincidence reappears again being that was the same way I felt listening to the Boss.

"You know why you and I are good together. Because we watch each other's back." A statement from his loyal friend Bubba during the height of the Viet Nam war. The connection between the nickname BaBa I had given my daughter did not connect with me until years later while looking back at my timeline.

THAT MIND OF OURS

"I ran for 7 years, 6 months, 13 days. I thought about Bubba, Lt. Dan, and Momma. I mostly thought about Jenny. "Forrest Gump. One of the many lines I recited out loud during my first 8-mile Spartan Race. Along with the many thoughts about the people in my own life I kept to myself.

"I'm not sure if life is supposed to be a path full of destiny. Or if it is fulfilled by the choices we make. I think it's a little of both." Forrest Gump in response to his mother's goodbye speech.

The Last Samurai. This movie happens to be the largest of a few movies posters I carried with me during my travels. Each poster was a reminder of what each movie stood for.

"Why do you continue to fight against your own kind?" "The sides may differ, Yet I will always fight for what I believe in." A conversation between a war solider played by Tom Cruise and his former commanding officer. Although I never considered myself being a Tom Cruise fan, I was impressed how well he portrayed a rebel in that movie. Part of me was intrigued by his role with his own book club called Scientology. Perhaps I too was being a bit of a rebel by hanging his picture when he wore his hair the longest. Years later the beloved and admirable Tom was interviewed on the Oprah show when he confessed his love for whoever his wife was at the time. The poster also served as a reminder just how quickly our society can turn on someone. It doesn't matter how lovable of a public figure someone is or even if they are a King. Which is reason one of my posters belong to Major League Baseball's Hit King. And to think, Tom's downfall was all because he got too excited expressing his new-found love for someone. In that sense, I suppose my book will never be feature on her book club show. I can only imagine what I might say or do on her couch if I got too excited expressing my love. Like all daytime talk shows, her show never interested me. Yet I found it very interesting that the name of her production studio is her name spelled backwards. Harpo. Although I never liked her as a talk show host, I found the roles she portrayed in movies to be most inspiring. With most Hollywood public personalities, I never paid regards to any facts about their lives off the screen. To me it was a disloyalty from the same sources that gave them images of grandeur. In fact, it just happened that I learned Oprah's interesting FYI while riding on a mob tour bus in Chicago. My interest in the mob has always been the same reason two of my movie posters belonged to The Godfather and The Sopranos. Their sense of loyalty. No matter how many rules of society a mobster broke, our society never

John B Lester

THAT MIND OF OURS

dared to bring down a boss. Especially not Mr. Bruce Springsteen, even if he did grow long hair. Nothing interests our society more than the mob. What interested me the most is how a mobster can admit involvement in multiple "Hits" and be glorified by society. Yet one All American Football athlete turned actor becomes accused of possibly killing his wife and her lover gets a yearlong trial and a society that hates him. That would be the reason his image is one of those posters that hang on my wall. A reminder that one is guilty until Oprah says your innocent. Later, in my life it served as a reminder how we were connected during my own trial and his second trial. Just one Las Vegas courtroom apart from one another. Even Hit King Pete Rose had a connection story worth sharing. My father talked about the time he went to Pete's restaurant in Boca Raton to watch the Super Bowl. Just after the game started he approached

John B Lester

THAT MIND OF OURS

Pete and asked him if he wanted to place a wager on the game with him. Despite being subjected to Pete's infamous yelling and backtalk he did not make my father leave his restaurant. About five later my father and I walked into the same restaurant. My father was excited to see Mr. Rose sitting down eating his lunch. We both looked over at the large printed sign hanging on the front door that read Absolutely No Pictures or Autographs Permitted or You Will Be Asked to Leave. He became flustered and anxiously took out his camera, while insisting to take our picture. At first I was reluctant until he edged me by saying "Come on. Don't be such a wimp." With that I headed over to Mr. Roses table and asked if the tall man standing near us with the big silly grin on his face could take our picture. He placed down his fork with irritation while giving me a stern disapproving look. He then snarled his question to me,

John B Lester

THAT MIND OF OURS

"Did you not read the big sign on the front door when you came in?" I gave him an animated gesture of cluelessness and told him I did read it. He shook his head while signing a postcard picture of himself. He looked up glaring at my father holding out his camera like a proud father was taking a picture of his son's first varsity wrestling match. Mr. Rose put on an awkward looking smile the best he could while I flexed my bicep over his head. He then quietly resumed his lunch. Neither one of us was asked to leave that day either.

Another movie that makes a notable recall on my time line was Swamp Thing. The story was based on a man reborn from the waters of Louisiana by a scientific formula. When the Swamp Thing is questioned how he found the formulas perfect combination, he replied. "It doesn't make you something better than you are. It only makes you more of what you are." Although in the end it was loved that saved him. Leaving the possibility that love in fact could have been the formulas secret ingredient.

In 2010, I remained in Las Vegas Nevada for the conclusion of my trial as well as the delivery of my first-born daughter. The mother to be and I took the place of my recently deceased father in the movie going department. A period when most of my spare time was spent visiting the Regal Cinema inside the Red Rock Hotel and Casino. Again, I became familiarized with all the current and upcoming movies. It would be a surprise that came from my child's mother to be. A mysterious DVD, one that I had never heard of. I pondered the reasons why such a well-made movie with big name actors would skip the big screen and go directly to DVD.

John B Lester

THAT MIND OF OURS

Limitless- "It's not a drug. It's unlike anything the world has ever known about." "It's the answers to everything." Although at that time I was far from having the answers to everything, it gave me the answer to one very important thing. It was the first time I believed my journey served a real purpose. Becoming a father was the most fearful thing I had to face during my lifetime. After that day, I no longer lived with the mentality of having nothing to lose. Instead I continued onward believing I had everything to gain. It was also the last time I recalled experiencing any type of fear. Even though I would not read Mark Twain's quote until years later, I find it most fitting to use here. "The two most important days in our lives are the day we are born and the day we find out what we were born to do." Something I place immense value in is the originality of a well written quote A few years later Limitless was turned into a spin off series starring a main character named Brian. Another reminder that my purpose was one worth being quotable.

Limitless Season 1- "I know this sounds crazy, but I believe this is something is making me the better person I always wanted to be."

My Voice: Indeed, I do credit you for being nothing other than original. Only I must take credit for leading you to those Limitless reminders. Except it was a reminder that could be summed up into just one word. And it was in the title that spoke for itself. Limitless.

My Voice: Some might say they believe life itself to be a game of politics. Yet you were correct to say that the answers have always been reachable to anyone who went searching for them. Even in your beloved comic books. Or to be politically correct, your beloved graphic novels.

John B Lester

THAT MIND OF OURS

My Mind: Apparently you read my mind, since DC comics is one of my upcoming chapters. Or did I read your mind? I am not sure of any politically correct way to put it.

My Voice: My question for you then is this. Do you relate more to a man of steel who flies over tall buildings or an iron man who runs faster than a speeding train?

My Mind: Very nice. A question we never talked about before, which means that is a genuine answer you seek. Quite easy, considering the way we met. The bird. If I was to relate to someone among the graphic novel world it would be an X man. One who is very much capable of experiencing pain. One who has the capacity to live many lifetimes. The X men series gave me a sense of comfort knowing there have been many other X men and many other Y women who have come to possess the gift I refer to as the XYZ factor. That reason being another one of the posters on my wall. The Justice League.

X-Men. The Apocalypse. – "Give man the gift of insight, he will learn to fear the world. Give man the gift of flight, he will fly to close to the sun. Give man the gift of all gifts, he will feel the need to rule the world

My Voice: Seems fitting that would make you the U man (human)

The Da Vinci Code. Author Dan Brown- "The holy grail has always been the bloodline. Hence, the last and final of my posters. True Blood.

The Mannequin- . A story how love brings a mannequin girl to life, while bringing love to a lifeless man. The mannequin's character would later evolve into the character Samantha in the groundbreaking series titled

John B Lester

THAT MIND OF OURS

Sex in the City. A role that showed the world there could be sex without love. Then later showed the world there could be love without sex. The movie's came with a theme song created by Starship. A very fitting title Nothing's Gonna Stop Us Now.

As I continue to re-read my own story I realize how this type of ending could be fitting for a King. In fact, it did become a fit ending for a King. Mr. Stephen King. The only King who never optioned to be glamorized in public. He maintained the ideal image of a true Ghostwriter. He remains the one King society has not dethroned Just who is this mystery King?. To me, his stories seemed to lack the proper ending. Perhaps the type of ending he himself was searching for. As I look back on my own timeline and think about love, fate, and destiny. I often think about the first time I met someone I called my soul mate. A time I had just began my career as a RN The actual time was around 2 00 am in a quiet cafeteria, at JFK hospital. Perhaps the reason Mr. Kings latest novel/miniseries was a personal favorite of mine.

11-22-63- A subtitle that reads If you could change history, would you want to. The story about a struggling author is given a time travel assignment to prevent JFK's assassination. During this time, he falls in love with a girl he hopes to be with forever. Only to find out that if he changes the course of history in any way, it will inevitably lead to her death. In the end, he makes the ultimate sacrifice to let her go so she can live a full life. Only then he realizes his assignment was never about changing JFK's outcome, it was about changing his own. Meanwhile as this part of the story comes to an end I take satisfaction knowing the King finally has an ending worth

John B Lester

THAT MIND OF OURS

reading. While I myself have a story worth sharing. As I said at the beginning. No matter which way I looked back on my own timeline, it was undoubtedly a love story.

John B Lester

THAT MIND OF OURS

A Publishing Philosophy Worth Promoting

Picture this. A writer's convention/workshop that delivers a unique ideology that merges self-publication with traditional publication. The specifics of what one can expect during and after they created their platform. By using examples of my personal trial and errors I plan to provide a unique perspective on how to pitch a book. I will provide the audience with guest speakers that pertain to the workshop. Giving the speakers a chance to share their own story. As well as allowing the audience to benefit from their services. My timeline of research inadvertently leads to the establishment of my own publishing company, which I plan on announcing at the

John B Lester

THAT MIND OF OURS

conference. The town resides over 250 local authors along with dozens of writer's special interest groups within its 50-mile radius

The event is a collaboration with the town's proactive Chamber of Commerce. The Florida Nurses Association, and even the town's tourism committee. There is talks of giving PG a new image using the iconic Ponce de Leon. And in case I may not have mentioned, my novel is based on the timeless adventures of Ponce de Leon.

Currently I am seeking out additional speakers and or vendor that may have their own story/services to share. My company will not pay these partners for their rights. Nor will I ask for any fees. The short-term goal is to promote each other's story so that we may each reach our projected goals A concept which promotes a win-win philosophy behind a company I call Team Prosper.

The Workshop Story

Life is a series of 2-minute dating. The first 10 Seconds is the initial glance. What is the first thing everyone notices? Male or female. The next 30 seconds determines if they want to know you. So, make an impression worth remembering.

The Hook- Also known as your book hook. "I am an open book. An artist. Willing to stand naked before my audience. Sharing with you my thoughts, my body, my story. Open minded. Open for judgement. Laugh at me or laugh with me."

John B Lester

THAT MIND OF OURS

You have 80 seconds remaining on your two-minute date to pitch yourself to give them an idea of who you are. Tell them a story worth remembering.

Travel nursing was more than just an adventure for me to see the world. It was a journey that allowed me to find a purpose. A way to help others. Along those roads I found someone worth helping. Even when all the odds were against me. I found way to love. Even if it meant receiving none in return.

By using a hook with sincerity, you will have completed a proper two-minute introduction. And if that isn't good enough to hold anyone's attention. You could always host your own workshop and take your time telling all the stories you want.

Family First. Research Second. Writing Third. In terms of math this equation could be simply balanced by finding the common denominator. Although my family might not be considered traditional, we always came together for our dinnertime traditions A time we made for each other, no matter how busy we were. Find the common denominator that bonds your group together and you will always have a story worth writing.

There are between **600,000** and **1,000,000 books** published every year in the US alone, depending on which stats you believe. Many of those – perhaps as many as half or even more – are self-published.

Source: Author's Earnings

How many books have ever been published in all of modern history? According to Google's advanced algorithms, the answer is nearly **130 million books**, or **129,864,880**, to be exact.

John B Lester

THAT MIND OF OURS

Source: Google

That means the amount of newly published books have more than tripled in the past three years. This means the desire for books and writers is still in high demand. Books have been one of our fundamentals tools in our growth development whether we realize it or not. Most people still eat their meals near a cookbook. Most people still base their values on what they learn from a Good Book. Most children still fall asleep to a fairy-tale book. And just about everyone still places value on a really good story.

.

John B Lester

THAT MIND OF OURS

At this point in time my story formatted itself nicely in the form of 200 pages and just a few words short of 20,000 words. Seems almost too fitting for a subtle way to end a book. Then a voice told me, A really good story never really comes to an end

A gentle reminder to myself.

John B Lester

THAT MIND OF OURS

"Never Let Other People's Perspective Limit Your Capabilities"

John B Lester

THAT MIND OF OURS

About the Author

John B Lester is a nurse by profession. A caregiver by nature. An adventurer at heart. And a storyteller with a purpose;

From an early age, long before I ever began my career in nursing I can still remember that burning desire to explore the things beyond which we were taught. To learn from the many cultures our world had to offer. A desire that led me to my path in travel nursing. One which started a journey of a lifetime. Within that journey, I learned mostly about the people I met and cared for. Those people taught me that kindness, laughter, and compassion was the universal caring that people needed the most. Those are the fundamental values that makes me proud to be a nurse/writer. No matter which path my future should lead to.

Places lived: New Jersey, Chicago, Boston, San Francisco, Las Vegas, Houston, Palm Beach.

Places Visited: The London Bridge, The Great Wall of China, Vietnam, Amsterdam, Cambodian Ruins, The Roman Colosseum, Dubai, The Egyptian Pyramids, Thailand, Mexico, Canada

John B Lester

THAT MIND OF OURS

Other Titles by John B Lester

The Story of Team Prosper

Turing's Wartime Story

Sharkey Malarkey's Adventure Home

A Divine Timeline

John B Lester

THAT MIND OF OURS

John B Lester

THAT MIND OF OURS

FIRST IMPRESSIONS

- LIFE IS A SERIES OF 2-MINUTE DATING. THE FIRST 10 SECONDS IS THE INITIAL GLANCE. WHAT IS THE FIRST THING EVERYONE NOTICES? MALE OR FEMALE. THE NEXT 30 SECONDS DETERMINES IF THEY WANT TO KNOW YOU. SO, MAKE AN IMPRESSION WORTH REMEMBERING.

- "I AM AN OPEN BOOK. AN ARTIST. WILLING TO STAND NAKED BEFORE MY AUDIENCE. SHARING WITH YOU MY THOUGHTS, MY BODY, MY STORY. OPEN MINDED. OPEN FOR JUDGEMENT. LAUGH AT ME OR LAUGH WITH ME."

- OTHERWISE KNOWN AS A BOOK'S INTRODUCTION

LAUGH WITH ME OR LAUGH AT ME......

- FROM AN EARLY AGE, LONG BEFORE I EVER BEGAN MY CAREER IN NURSING I CAN STILL REMEMBER THAT BURNING DESIRE TO EXPLORE THE THINGS BEYOND WHICH WE WERE TAUGHT. TO LEARN FROM THE MANY CULTURES OUR WORLD HAD TO OFFER. A DESIRE THAT LED ME TO MY PATH IN TRAVEL NURSING. ONE WHICH STARTED A JOURNEY OF A LIFETIME. WITHIN THAT JOURNEY, I LEARNED MOSTLY ABOUT THE PEOPLE I MET AND CARED FOR. THOSE PEOPLE TAUGHT ME THAT KINDNESS, LAUGHTER, AND COMPASSION WAS THE UNIVERSAL CARING THAT PEOPLE NEEDED THE MOST. THOSE ARE THE FUNDAMENTAL VALUES THAT MAKES ME PROUD TO BE A NURSE NO MATTER WHICH PATH MY FUTURE SHOULD LEAD TO.

- OTHERWISE KNOWN AS A BOOK HOOK

John B Lester

THAT MIND OF OURS

WHAT MOTIVATES YOU TO WRITE/S.P.

01 Recognition- To see your story on the cover of a book?

02 Income- a way to semi retire from your daily job or land a nicely paid contract?

03 Legacy- to ensure your story is passed down the way you want it to be?

04 Pure passion and desire to write your story?

A THOUGHT WORTH CONSIDERING

J.D. Salinger was said to have a mentor at the start of his career. Salinger was asked if he knew he might write for the rest of his life without ever receiving anything in return. Would he still want to be a writer? He would eventually write one of Americas greatest known novel The Catcher in the Rye. Ironically his career would end there. Spending the rest of his life writing in solitaire. His only known writing was a letter to his mentor years later which read. Yes, I would spend the rest of my life writing with nothing in return. There are reasons certain well-known writers are placed in a league of their own. You know them as the same top 12 names listed under any search engine on the internet. Commonly known for their disturbed personalities. All sharing one thing in common. They were all searching for a connection. Inevitably for a way to connect with their readers. Eventually earning them the reputations as the immortalized authors they are remembered as today Those unique individuals searched for something which could not be explained to them. Perhaps the reason many people choose not to search for something of that magnitude. It can be frightening. And people are frightened by things that can't be explained.

John B Lester

THAT MIND OF OURS

THE FIRST STORYBOOK

* AN EMERGING INVESTMENT COMPANY NAMED PROSPER ANNOUNCED MY STORY AS THE TOP ENTRY FOR THEIR HOLIDAY CONTEST. IT WAS THE FIRST TIME MY WRITING HAD BEEN GIVEN A SENSE OF VALIDATION. SHORTLY AFTERWARDS I CONNECTED WITH A SMALL TEAM OF ILLUSTRATORS FROM THE OTHER SIDE OF THE WORLD. A PLACE NAMED INDIA. TOGETHER, WE TURNED THAT STORY INTO OUR FIRST PUBLICATION NAMED THE STORY OF TEAM PROSPER. A STORY ON HOW THE BEST INVESTMENT BEGINS WHEN WE INVEST IN OURSELVES. AND BEGINS TO PROSPER ONCE WE BELIEVE IN OURSELVES

WRITING FOR THE BIG PICTURE

- WHO WILL FIND A 24 PAGE HOLIDAY BOOK BY AN UNKNOWN WRITER?
- WRITE A MOVIE FOR THE WORLD TO BECOME KNOWN.
- WRITE A BOOK FOR MY FATHER WORTH REMEMBERING.

MY PLATFORM

- AN APPROACH TO PITCH MY STORYBOOK
- TRIAL AND ERROR BOOK FOR THE BEST PUBLICATION METHOD
- INCLUDE A FEW GOOD STORIES ALONG THE WAY
- MY TRIAL WITH OJ SIMPSON - THAT ONE FOR ANOTHER BOOK

John B Lester

THAT MIND OF OURS

NOTABLES FROM MY FIRST WORKSHOP

- Make It Personal.
- Speakers lasting impression
- My Personal Thank You Letter

- My "Pitch" Experience
- 4 Strikes. No love finds romance group

- There is no longer any "Right" way.
- Heads or Tails- 50% chance to be right yet wrong 70%

WE HAVE TIME. ALL THE TIME IN THE WORLD

- HOW MUCH TIME DOES ONE HAVE TO WRITE
- WRITING TO PLATFORM YOUR AUDIENCE

FROM SELF DOUBT TO NO DOUBT

I BEGAN WRITING MY PERSONAL STORY AND MY STORY FOR THE MOVIES AT THE SAME TIME. THE ADVENTURES OF PONCE DE LEON WHICH WOULD INCORPORATE 500 YEARS OF HISTORY. A GOOD PLATFORM FOR THE LOCALS, EDUCATION, AND ADVENTURE FANS OF ALL AGES.

A BOOK IS NOT JUDGE BY ITS COVER

HIGH PRICE COVER DESIGNS
COVERS SHOULD BE THOUGHT PROVOKING MORE THAN EYE CATCHING

PAID REVIEWS
A REVIEW SHOULD ONLY BE A PENNY FOR A THOUGHT

PAID AGENT SESSIONS
JUST LIKE ANY PROPOSAL IT SHOULD BE A TWO WAY INTERVIEW

John B Lester

THAT MIND OF OURS

TRADITIONAL VS SELF PUBLISHING

This route requires a detailed one page query letter. Your story formatted to each publishers submission requirements. Found on any publishers submission page. There you will also find out if they allow author submission or only accept submission by your agent. replies take a minimum 6-10 weeks.

Should a contract be offered- 5-15k sign on offer for the rights of your book. They handle edits, marketing, distribution, and eBook conversions.

After 10-20 k copies sold you will receive royalties for each additional copy sold. Approx.. $1.15

Carries an air of importance and bragging rights of being published

TOWN BOOK PROPOSAL

- A win win concept for every writer in any town
- The chamber connection
- My trip adviser story

THAT MIND OF OURS

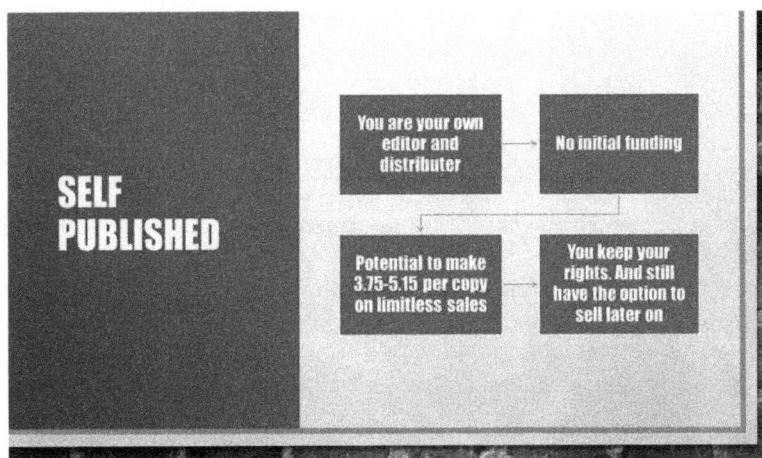

SELF PUBLISHED

- You are your own editor and distributer
- No initial funding
- Potential to make 3.75-5.15 per copy on limitless sales
- You keep your rights. And still have the option to sell later on

NUMBERS NEVER LIE

- THERE ARE BETWEEN 600,000 AND 1,000,000 BOOKS PUBLISHED EVERY YEAR IN THE US ALONE, DEPENDING ON WHICH STATS YOU BELIEVE. MANY OF THOSE – PERHAPS AS MANY AS HALF OR EVEN MORE – ARE SELF-PUBLISHED.
- 2016- 300,000 TRADITIONAL PUBLISHED BOOKS: 700,000 SELF PUBLISHED BOOKS
- SOURCE: AUTHOR'S EARNINGS
- HOW MANY BOOKS HAVE EVER BEEN PUBLISHED IN ALL OF MODERN HISTORY? ACCORDING TO GOOGLE'S ADVANCED ALGORITHMS, THE ANSWER IS NEARLY 130 MILLION BOOKS, OR 129,864,880, TO BE EXACT.
- SOURCE GOOGLE

John B Lester

THAT MIND OF OURS

RESOURCES

- Create space-no cost/low cost. Great learning tools
- Eventbrite.com
- Ingram.com
- Amazon author

INGRAM BLOG & TOOLS

- ADVANCE READER COPIES, OR SOMETIMES CALLED ADVANCE REVIEW COPIES OR GALLEYS (BUT FREQUENTLY SHORTENED TO ARCS), ARE ADVANCE COPIES OF YOUR BOOK THAT YOU OFFER TO BOOKSELLERS, BOOK REVIEWERS, POTENTIAL MEDIA OUTLETS, THOSE YOU'RE ASKING FOR ENDORSEMENTS FOR YOUR BOOK, ETC. PREPUBLICATION. PREPUBLICATION IS THE IMPORTANT PIECE HERE. THESE EARLY COPIES ARE PART OF A BOOK MARKETING STRATEGY TO HELP YOU BUILD EXCITEMENT FOR YOUR BOOK BEFORE IT'S PUBLISHED.
- COST CALCULATOR
- TRIM/FILE REQUIREMENTS FOR PRINT BOOKS

John B Lester

THAT MIND OF OURS

NON ONLINE MARKETING

BOOKSTORES
MOST BOOK STORES WILL STOCK YOUR BOOK FOR 50 ONE TIME FEE
BENEFITS COME FROM MONTHLY EVENTS
LOCAL AUTHOR SIGNINGS
CHILDREN'S STORY TIME GROUPS

DIVERSE CULTURES
NATIVE AMERICAN TRIBES
JEHOVAH WITNESS
PHILIPPIAN GROUPS
BOOK TRANSLATION SERVICES

LOCAL EVENTS
CHAMBER OF COMMENCE MEMBER
CONCERTS/TRADE SHOWS
LIBRARIES
RELIGIOUS CENTERS
SCHOOLS
ALLIANCE ARTS

THROW IN A LITTLE LOVE AND GREAT FOOD BETWEEN THE BOOKS

THEN CAME MAHAL'S KITCHEN

FROM VENDOR TO CONVENTION
THE BIG STEPUP WAS ACTUALLY 333 STEPS

John B Lester

THAT MIND OF OURS

DISTRIBUTION AND VENDOR PLANNING. HAVING A BUSINESS PLAN

- Ein number
- Sunbiz registration
- Business account
- Duns filing
- Supplier number

ISBN & COPYRIGHTS

* ISBN REQUIRED IF YOU INTEND TO SELL YOUR BOOK. ANY ITEM YOU BUY FROM A STORE HAS A PRODUCT NUMBER ASSOCIATED WITH IT TO IDENTIFY THE ITEM YOU'RE PURCHASING. AND BOOKS ARE NO DIFFERENT. YOUR ISBN IS YOUR PRODUCT NUMBER AND IT'S UNIQUE TO YOUR BOOK AND YOUR BOOK ALONE. AND NOT ONLY DOES IT IDENTIFY YOUR BOOK, IT ALSO IDENTIFIES THE SPECIFIC FORMAT OF YOUR BOOK, INDICATING WHETHER IT'S THE PAPERBACK, HARDCOVER, OR EBOOK VERSION. YOU SHOULD ALSO BE WARY OF ACCEPTING ISBNS FOR "FREE". IT'S BEST TO OWN YOUR OWN ISBN AS A SELF-PUBLISHER.

John B Lester

THAT MIND OF OURS

THE TRUTH OF THE MATTER

* THE AMOUNT OF NEWLY PUBLISHED BOOKS HAVE MORE THAN TRIPLED IN THE PAST THREE YEARS. THIS MEANS THE DESIRE FOR BOOKS AND WRITERS ARE STILL IN HIGH DEMAND. BOOKS ARE STILL PART OF OUR FUNDAMENTAL GROWTH DEVELOPMENT. MOST PEOPLE STILL EAT THEIR MEALS NEAR A COOKBOOK. MANY PEOPLE STILL BASE THEIR VALUES FROM THE GOOD BOOK. CHILDREN STILL FALL ASLEEP TO FAIRY-TALE BOOKS.

PITCHING LIKE AN ACE

STORY MARKETING-PITCHING BETWEEN THE LINES

Father & Son Pitching Story

MLB PLAYERS STRIKE OUT 70% OF THE TIME AND ARE STILL CONSIDERED A STAR

John B Lester

THAT MIND OF OURS

COLLABORATE WITH OTHER INDUSTRIES

- Workshops/public presentations
- Professional healthcare-offer ceu
- Online workshop-Eventbrite
- Adult learning centers, technical schools, community colleges

John B Lester

THAT MIND OF OURS

DEFINING A TRUE HERO

* SOMETIME DURING THE 1990'S MY FATHER TOOK ME TO A YANKEE-RED SOX GAME. OUR FIRST INTRODUCTION TO A ROOKIE PITCHER NAMED JON LESTER. HIS NAME WAS ALSO JOHN LESTER.
* A FEW YEARS LATER THAT POTENTIAL STAR WAS STRICKEN WITH CANCER.
* HIS RETURN WOULD BECOME ONE OF BASEBALL'S GREATEST COMEBACK STORIES EVER.
* OVER THE YEARS WHENEVER THIS ACE WAS SCHEDULED TO PITCH MY FATHER AND I WOULD CALL EACH OTHER SAYING "GUESS WHAT, WE ARE PITCHING TONIGHT" GIVING US SOMETHING WORTH TALKING ABOUT
* AFTER MY FATHER PASSED I LOST MY INTEREST IN WATCHING THE WINNING DYNASTIES PLAY
* INSTEAD I BECAME HOPEFUL OF THE INFAMOUS UNDERDOGS, THE CHICAGO CUBS
* IN 2016 I MODELED MY PROSPECTIVE COMPANY USING THE CUBBIES ROYAL BLUE COLORS
* EACH WRITING SESSION I WOULD TELL MY FATHER "THIS IS GOING TO BE THE YEAR OF THE ROYAL BLUE UNDERDOGS"
* AFTER ALL IT WAS THE YEAR THE CUBS ACQUIRED THEIR ACE PICHER, JON LESTER

KEEP DREAMING

MY WHOLE LIFE PEOPLE ALWAYS TOLD ME TO "KEEP DREAMING"

SO I DID

John B Lester

THAT MIND OF OURS

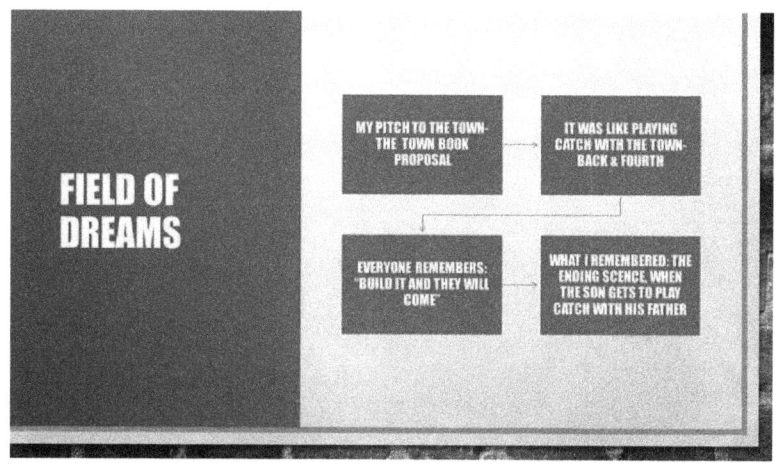

A WRITERS PRAYER

Perhaps somewhere along my timeline was a writers prayer.

The 12 characters in a mid summer dream. Apostles Creed

The long shot final pitch. The Hail Mary

Or just a story for Our Father

A REASON TO BELIEVE

- EVERY STORY HAS MORE THAN ONE MEANING
- WHAT MY STORY MEANS TO ME. IT GAVE ME REASON TO BELIEVE
- TO BELIEVE IN MYSELF "NEVER LET OTHERS PEOPLE EXPECTATIONS LIMIT YOUR CAPABILITY"
- TO BELIEVE IN SPIRITS. THERE IS NO BETTER SPIRIT THAN A TEAM SPIRIT
- TO BELIEVE IN A HIGHER POWER MAKES A POWERFUL MIND.

John B Lester

THAT MIND OF OURS

MORE THAN A TITLE

Over six months I couldn't believe how much the timeline of histories greatest influences collated with my own timeline.

Did my subconscious have a higher iq than my conscious?

Do we really know just how powerful a mind can be?

The title for this movie . That I had absolutely no doubt.

A DIVINE TIMELINE

THAT MIND OF OURS

LOYALTIES ARE WORTH THAN ROYALTIES

Thank you. All those who believed in my story and gave me a reason to believe.

The workshop that would give back to the community

A LEGENDARY PIRATE RETURNS HOME

THE STORY BEHIND JOSE GASPAR AND THE ISLAND OF GASPARILLA

John B Lester

THAT MIND OF OURS

THE BIG PICTURE
- Writing For the Big Screen to The Bigger Picture
- Healthcare & Educational Writing
- Political Reforms & Lobbying Letters
- Things That Mean Much More – Higher Understanding

A PENNY FOR MY AFTERTHOUGHTS

- More stories about the people I met along my own timeline
- My trial with OJ
- That would be another pitch
- Not the final pitch. Because a truly good story never really ends

John B Lester

THAT MIND OF OURS

THAT MIND OF OURS

ADDING VALUE TO CLOSING THOUGHTS

NO RIGHT WAY STILL REQUIRES THE RIGHT PHILOSOPHY

John B Lester

THAT MIND OF OURS

> Whether this story gets played on the silver screen for everyone to see. Or remains inside the family vault for my children to one-day view. Here are some closing thoughts I try and remind myself about life. If it was a personal prison you sentenced me to, I gave you my full disclosure. If your fear tactics were meant to intimidate me, I showed you what true courage is capable of. If you were looking to change me, I adapted, while staying true to my beliefs. If you wished to ridicule me, I showed you how to find laughter in yourself. If you meant was drive me insane, I showed you that there was nothing more crazy than true love. If it was a hero you hoped for, I gave you a way to save others. And if it was gratitude you were looking for, I showed you how to live gratefully with simplicity. This is my message to everyone, from That Mind of Mine.

MY REVISED "PITCHING AN AGENT" SECTION

- Giving value for clients dollar
- Making connections instead of getting customers

John B Lester

THAT MIND OF OURS

TEA FOR TWO SESSIONS

- This is our company's version of critique or pitch opportunity
- It's gives us a chance to meet and personalize your experience
- Questions and feedback
- Submit your story to be part of our tour team
- I will offer ways to better your self publishing experience and or your story
- Your story will be delivered to a review panel of authors. You will have at least 6 reviews to post on your website or book

FLORIDA NURSE ASSOCIATION

Florida Nurse Association as a constituent of the American Nurses Association is the only nursing organization representing ALL of nursing regardless of specialty or practice area. We speak on behalf of nursing in Tallahassee as well as before many regulatory bodies. We partner with other organizations that share our vision to create a unified nursing advocacy program for nurses in our state.

Members may apply for funding for projects and activities

John B Lester

THAT MIND OF OURS

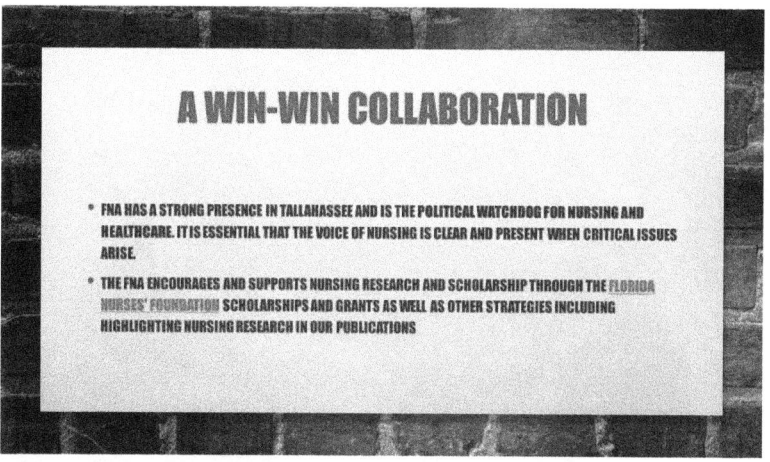

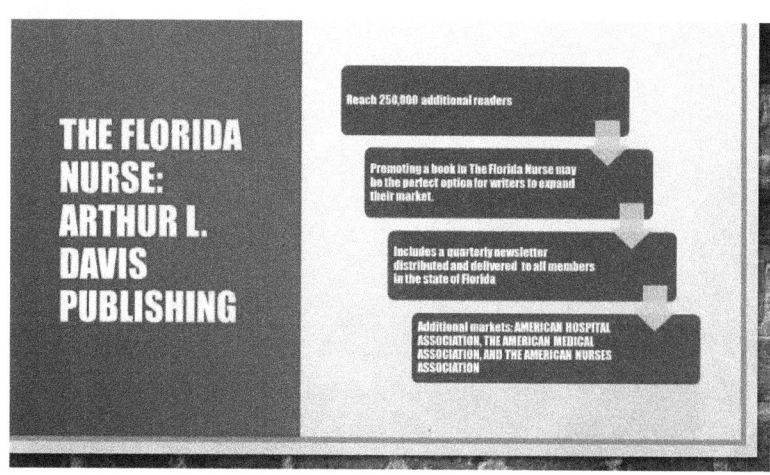

www.ingramcontent.com/pod-product-compliance
Lightning Source LLC
Chambersburg PA
CBHW051753040426
42446CB00007B/343